Mysterious Missouri

"Show-Me" the Strange Stuff

by Ross Malone

Bluebird Publishing Co.
8220 Exchange Way
St. Louis MO 63144
www.Bluebirdbookpub.com

Introduction

When I was your age I used to love the stories of unexplained things. Friends told ghost stories in the dark, television had Science Fiction Theater, and the folks in my Ozarks community always had strange stories to pass on to willing listeners. Yes, I did love those thought-provoking stories. And I still do!

I hope you will find some smiles and some goose bumps in the stories that follow. As my grandkids read these, the most common comment I hear is probably "Ewwwwwww!" That's good. Scary stuff, strange stuff, and gross stuff should make us feel that "Ewwwwwww!" response.

I was asked to write this book because there seems to be no good book for kids that concentrates on the mysterious and strange things about the Show-Me State. All parts of Missouri have their own legends and unexplained happenings – and lots of them! I've tried to write about some of my favorites.

Since there are so many stories coming from all over, I have not been able to include them all. Do you know of a good story that's not in the book? If you know a good one, gather all the details you can and send them to me by e-mail. Maybe I'll use your story in my next book. If I do, I'll list your first name and your county on the contributor's page of the book.

Thanks for reading my stories. I hope you enjoy them!

Ross W. Malone
RnDMalone@att.net

Credits

I want to thank Steven LaChance and all of the others who have helped me to put these stories together. Special thanks go to those who have contributed some of the photographs on these pages.

Joe Sonderman did some wonderful research by pouring through old newspapers and putting the information on line for us to use. I have selected some of Joe's gleanings and included them here. You will especially see this in the section on the St. Louis World's Fair.

The Missouri Department of Conservation gave me the idea for one of these articles. They carried a Halloween spoof about zombies in the great out-of-doors and I just had to pass it along. They do good work for us and sometimes they provide us with some clever good humor.

Those who asked me to do this book deserve some special thanks and my family who tolerated me sharing all of these stories as they came together. I appreciate you!

Table of Contents

Strange Animals

MoMo the Missouri Monster

When I thought about writing this book the very first thing that came to mind was the famous Missouri Monster known as MoMo. After all, this thing had a ride named for it at Six Flags. A "concrete" ice cream treat at Ted Drewes named the MoMo, a song was written, and now a movie is being made, so it's pretty famous. I decided to start with MoMo because there are some things we can learn from him about monsters and mysteries.

Momo is supposed to be similar to the Bigfoot, except this one doesn't live in the high mountiains. MoMo is reported to live in Missouri. The name Momo is short for 'Missouri Monster.' This one is said to have a large, pumpkin-shaped head, with a furry body, and hair covering the eyes. He is famous for eating dogs and for his terrible stinking fur. Some say they have heard him scream like a panther. Some say that he makes gurgling noises.

First reported in July 1971, near Louisiana, Missouri by two young women, Momo has been spotted in many places but always pretty close to the Mississippi River. The young women said that MoMo came out of the woods and, when they ran for their car, he stole their picnic lunch. They said MoMo was about 7 ft tall, with black fur, and looked sort of like a man. Some suggest it was a rogue black bear.

Three children claimed to see the monster in 1972 and once again, it was in July. The kids said that he walked past them carrying a dead dog. They assumed it was for his meal. Why else would you carry a dead dog around? There were other sightings for about 2 weeks. One farmer said that he didn't see the monster but he heard him growling and smelled that terrible stink. Another farmer said his dog was missing. Tracks were found and submitted to authorities. Hunters, fishermen, and motorists on Highway 79 continued to file reports with the police. In all, MoMo was seen in 29 Missouri counties.

Of course people from everywhere were coming to Louisiana and the area trying to find out more about this creature. Some said that it must be a type of "Big Foot" or Sasquatch. Others said it resembled descriptions of aliens from space and suggested that maybe there was a crashed spacecraft to be found. No one knew for sure but there were lots of interesting ideas to think about.

One day a twenty-man sheriff's posse was looking for MoMo when they found dog bones scattered around a little shack. The shack had a pile of leaves in one corner that looked like it might be a bed or a nest for the creature. Then they smelled that terrible smell. However, they couldn't find MoMo or any other living creature.

Some people enjoyed having MoMo around. A radio host in Bowling Green, Missouri wrote and recorded a song about the creature. In Louisiana, MO where he was first seen, they began to celebrate MoMo Days. On those special days people would wear wigs with the long hair hanging over their faces and the stores in town would put special bargains on sale. There was even a contest for the school kids to paint store windows and draw pictures of what they thought the monster looked like.

Then came the day when MoMo should have died. You see, some high school boys came forward and explained that they had been sitting up on Star Hill and feeling rather bored.

These bright and clever boys decided to do something to create some excitement. One of them remembered an old fake fur coat in his mother's closet so they got it and took turns wearing it to frighten people.

One boy found a dead dog and told his friend to carry it that day so people began to believe that the creature liked to eat dogs. The boys had good imaginations but so did the other people. Everyone's imaginations ran wild and anything unusual began to be blamed on MoMo. When the boys confessed everyone should have laughed and said that was the end of the monster – but they didn't.

People didn't want the monster to be gone. The stores wanted to have sales and the man on the radio wanted to sell his records. People continued to come to Louisiana because they wanted to believe that strange and mysterious things still happen in our modern world. So the legend of MoMo has been kept alive.

Up in the very first paragraph I said, "…there are some things we can learn from him about monsters and mysteries." Here are some of those things. First, it's fun to be scared. That's why we go on roller-coasters and visit spook houses on Halloween. We watch vampire movies and read zombie stories because it's fun to be scared.

Second, one of the best things about being human is that we have such wonderful imaginations. When we watch a movie or read a good book, it's fun to let our imaginations go. It's almost like living an adventure and that's also true with these mysteries.

The third thing is that you have to be careful when you look for the truth. You can search the internet for days and find all sorts of things about MoMo before you ever stumble across the story of the boys who created the hoax. People would rather write about the monster than about the truth so there is lots of fiction about scary things and not much fact.

The fourth thing is also important. We don't know everything. Just over one hundred years ago people thought the mountain gorilla didn't exist. Then in 1902 the legend turned out to be true. They weren't a myth at all – they were real. When Lewis and Clark first explored in Missouri and westward, they discovered 122 new animals. Just last year twelve new species were discovered around the world including inflatable sharks and rodent-eating plants. There are certainly things still waiting to be discovered and truths to be revealed.

Strange Houses

A house is never silent in darkness
to those who listen intently;
there is a whispering in distant chambers,
an unearthly hand presses the snib of the window,
the latch rises.
Ghosts were created when the first man
woke in the night.
* Sir James Matthew Barrie

The Noisy Farmhouse

When this writer was very young my family lived in a nice old farmhouse in Laclede County. I remember it as a big two-story house on a dusty gravel road very much like thousands of other houses across the state. But this one wasn't just like the others. You see, strange things happened in this one.

The first problem that my family encountered was a rocking chair that rocked when no one was near it. My parents assumed that it must be a breeze or a draft so they put some books and boxes in the chair hoping that the extra weight would stop the noisy rocking and let us get a better night's sleep. It didn't.

The chair continued to rock during the night until my father placed some bricks under the rockers so it couldn't possibly rock – he thought. Somehow that chair continued to rock through much of the night. Then came other nighttime noises.

One noise was worse than the others. At night there seemed to be a good deal of foot traffic on the stairs between the first and second floors. My family could never see anyone but the noise of feet going up and down those stairs was very clear.

I was so young that I don't remember many of the details about that place but the noises were enough to make my parents begin looking for another house. We did move and as time went by I noticed a long succession of people moving into that farmhouse and then moving quickly away. In fact I can't recall a single family that stayed there for more than a few weeks.

I did ask my uncle who lived nearby what he knew about the place and he said that it was built by a man who just went insane. Even he didn't live there for very long. My uncle had also noticed that no one stayed for very long but he didn't know why.

When something happens to you that can't be explained, you really don't want to tell everyone about it, do you? People might think you're a little crazy. I believe that's just what was happening in that house. Strange things happened to lots of people but no one wanted to talk about those things.

When I was a young man there were two final chapters in the life of that creepy place. One happened on a warm summer day when a neighbor man and his son were driving into Lebanon to buy some cattle feed. A new family had moved into the old farmhouse and the neighbor looked over that way planning to wave to the neighbors as farm people always do. It was then that the man and his son saw something they will never forget for the rest of their lives.

In the ditch next to the gravel road laid the father of the new family and his two daughters. They were alive but laid there covered by a very thick layer of dust from the road. All three were completely naked and out of their minds. The mother of the family sat on the front porch in a rocking chair, also completely naked and completely insane. Shortly after that, the empty house burned completely to the ground and the mysterious events came to an end.

To this day I know of a few people who remember some of the events surrounding the spooky old place but none of them will talk about it with strangers. We wouldn't want people to think we're crazy would we?

The Little Mansion

Several years ago a nice young family that I know was looking for a home in Dent County. There were some very nice little houses available but the family couldn't afford any of them. Then someone suggested another house that always seemed to be available. The young family hadn't looked at it because it was a big beautiful home with a nice lawn and shady old trees. It must be way too expensive for them!

When an agent showed them through the house they saw that many of the doors were made of beveled glass and the doorknobs were made of crystal. The big high-ceiling rooms had chandeliers hanging from them and hardwood floors. Everything was perfect. The most surprising thing was that this house cost much less than even the smallest of the other places. The young family quickly paid a deposit and made plans to move in. It was a dream come true – or a nightmare.

For a while, everything went well and the young couple settled into their new jobs, the baby girl and the big lovable dog played in the spacious yard, and the neighbors were nice. Then something began to change but none of them could say just what it was that changed. It was just something different in the mood or the atmosphere of the house.

The young mother said she got goose bumps whenever she tried to store anything in or take anything from the attic. "I can't tell you why," she said. "I just get this really creepy feeling when I go up those steps." She felt so strongly that she actually became afraid to even go near the attic stairs.

Her husband didn't feel so afraid of the attic but he did agree that some strange things happened there. Sometimes the attic would become extremely cold but they blamed the big oak trees outside. They thought the trees must keep the sun from warming the roof and the attic. Later they found that the attic could even be cold on hot summer days.

One hot and humid Saturday afternoon the young man was looking through some boxes when the attic became so cold that he decided to go downstairs and get a coat or jacket. When he got his coat and thought about being so cold on such a hot day, he decided not to go back up there that day.

A young woman who was babysitting at the house reported that she kept hearing steps in the house but no one was there. She also said that someone was knocking on the front door and ringing the doorbell but she could see the entire porch and no one was there.

The young couple told me of other strange happenings there but the one that really impressed me was the story of one evening when the little family was spending a quiet night at home. Mom and Dad were sitting on the living room sofa watching a favorite television program. The baby girl was in front of them playing with some soft toys on the floor. Bart, the big family dog, was lying next to the baby and seemed to be taking a nap.

Then, all at once, the baby's head lifted and the dog sat up. Both the baby and the dog stared at something on the east side of the room near the ceiling. The parents looked but could see nothing. Then the baby and the dog continued to stare and together their heads moved and their eyes followed the *something* around the top of the wall to the south side of the room above the parents.

With their heads still slowly moving and their eyes seeming to stare at the very same invisible something, the baby and the dog watched as the thing went from the top of the south wall to the top of the west wall. Then, whatever it was seemed to have gone up the stairs toward the attic and the dog laid back down and closed his eyes. The baby went back to playing with the toys as if nothing at all had happened. The parents could not figure out what the baby and the dog had seen.

This writer has visited that house many times and I have never seen anything unusual. The young family lived there for a few years and never had any problems. But they did stay out of the attic as much as possible. They felt that there was a friendly spirit sharing the house with them and they were OK with that.

The Screaming House in Union

A family I have known for years had an experience that changed their lives forever. Steven had three children, all in their early teen years. At one time they spotted a very nice two-story frame house for rent and they felt like it was just what they needed. Moving to this house from a smaller place would be great for the family. Each of them would have their own room, it was in the middle of the small town and everything was within easy walking-distance. A park, a swimming pool, and the Middle School were all nearby. There was even a nearby A & W root beer place where teenagers liked to hang out. For many reasons this was going to be a terrific new home for the family.

As the family moved in they weren't surprised when some neighbors came by. Neighbors often greet new-arrivers with words of welcome. These neighbors however, said things like, "We hope you get along OK here." That seemed a little strange.

Soon the family noticed other things. Pictures that hung on the wall wouldn't stay there. Neighbors crossed the street to avoid walking near the house. A big dark "something" chased the children from the basement. Then two weeks after moving in, Steven saw what he described as a dark figure of a man who seemed to be made of a "…moving, churning, dark gray and black smoke or mist." The figure came into the room with Steven and then just faded away.

Steven decided to leave the house and visit his parents. There he might have a chance to figure out what just happened. He quickly ushered his family out to the car and as they left, his son said, "Daddy, the basement monster is standing in the upstairs window."

After staying a short time with his parents, Steven took his family back to the house and things seemed to be fine for a while. Then one evening Steven was on the telephone when the inside doors began to rattle. All of a sudden Steven says the temperature dropped thirty degrees in the room and what felt like electricity ran through his body. A horrible nasty smell filled the room and then a screaming was heard upstairs.

Heavy steps boomed down the stairs as the screaming voice of a man got louder and the entire house began to shake. Steven grabbed for the children and they all ran to the car. They stopped a short distance away and watched as something dark went from room to room through the house as if it was looking for someone. Them?

The children never did go back to the house. But Steven did – to gather up some of their possessions. His brother and his father went with him on that trip. While there, his brother snapped some pictures. Steven's father later told me about that day's experiences in which they couldn't control the drastic changes in temperature of the house. He said that he had never believed in paranormal activities until that day.

When the pictures from that day were developed, a shadowy man appeared standing near Steven in one photo. He seemed to be a man from long ago with "mutton-chop" sideburns and a ribbon bow necktie. His face appeared very angry.

Later, research on the internet turned up the story of Captain John T. Crowe, a Civil War soldier who had lived in that very house. The picture on the internet looks very similar to the picture taken by Steven's brother.

House Similar to the
"Screaming House"
(The actual "Screaming House" is
not shown due
to consideration for the present
owners.)

At the time of this writing, no one lives in the house. If this story interests you or if you would like to know more about what has happened at the house over the last hundred years or so, read Steven A. LaChance's book, *The Uninvited: The True Story of the Union Screaming House.*

The Lemp Mansion

At one time there were three families in St. Louis who owned big breweries. The biggest and richest of all was the Lemp family. But we often see that being rich doesn't mean being happy. Over the years there were many unhappy events in the lives of the Lemp family and some say the results of that tragic sadness still live within the walls of their beautiful 33-room mansion.

The Lemp Mansion in 1892

In 1901 Frederick Lemp died under "mysterious circumstances" at the mansion. Three years later, Frederick's father, William J. went up to his bedroom and shot himself in the head. In 1919 the Prohibition Act closed the breweries all across America and the Lemp family no longer had their fabulous income but they still had plenty of money left over from the glory years.

Then in 1920 Elsa Lemp, the richest young woman in St. Louis committed suicide. In 1922 the family sold its brewery, which covered ten city blocks, to a shoe company. But with this sale, the Lemps were no longer involved in the brewing business. Even though they no longer worked in South St. Louis, they kept living there in the sad but beautiful old mansion.

After the brewery was sold, the company president, William Lemp Jr. felt so bad that he too went to the mansion and shot himself in the head just as his father had done eighteen years earlier. That left the family of William Lemp Jr.'s brothers Charles and Edwin and William Jr.'s son, William III.

William III, died of a heart attack in 1943 and that left only Uncle Charles living in the house by himself. Uncle Charles was a sad and bitter old man who kept to himself and didn't want other people coming to the mansion. Then, wouldn't you know, in 1949 he shot his dog and then shot himself in the head. He was found by his brother, Edwin.

At age ninety, Edwin died and that was the end of the fabulously wealthy and extremely sad family in the Lemp Mansion. While they lived in the mansion the family collected so much fine art that they couldn't display it all on their walls or in their gardens so they built a storage building behind the house. Later they had to build a second storage building because they were continuing to collect so much art. When

Edwin died his final order was to destroy his art collection and all of the family heirlooms. What a loss!

Today many people claim that the beautiful old house is still haunted by the spirits of the sad family from days gone by. In 1980 Life Magazine declared that the Lemp Mansion was one of the ten most haunted houses in America. In addition to the other people who died there, there are also reports of a "monkey-faced boy" who lives there in spirit form.

A young couple who were married in the mansion also spent their first night there. They told me of strange sounds all around but, of course that could have been people playing tricks on them. However, they also reported strange lights (orbs?) in their room. They said also that, even though the heat was turned up, the room was so cold that they could see their breath.

So, what makes this place seem to be haunted? Noises for one. People have reported hearing other people talk to them when no one seemed to be there. Other folks have reported hearing animals and birds. Visitors have told of hearing a dog bark and then feeling the dog brush up against them but they never see a dog. Some say that candles seem to light themselves and dinner guests have reported that table cloths were jerked off the tables but no one seemed to be there.

Smells are also present there. Some people report the smell of cigar smoke and others report lavender perfume. Some have reported the entire house being suddenly filled with a terrible stinking odor. Many people have reported having small personal items disappear even while they were in the room.

The most common thing reported in the mansion appears in photographs. Many people have reported that their cameras and their film seem to be alright before and after being in the Lemp Mansion and some are fine while there. But then they notice that some of their pictures (always in certain rooms) have little floating "orbs" in them. These little spots apparently can't be seen by us but they show up in the pictures we take.

You can visit the Lemp Mansion if you call ahead for reservations. You see, it is now a fancy restaurant and many people go there for the good food and for the chance to see or feel something strange. Sometimes, after the dinner guests have finished eating, the staff performs a murder mystery play. It's the perfect place for such a thing. Local radio personalities try to stay all night sometimes and they make it very entertaining.

Some fancy restaurants advertise their "fine wines and spirits." Here, it means something completely different. Most restaurants do a lot more business around certain holidays – especially Mother's Day and Valentines Day. The Lemp Mansion also does a lot of holiday business – at Halloween!

The Missouri Governor's Mansion

Missouri has had several capital buildings in St. Louis, St. Charles, and three in Jefferson City. So it's not surprising that we have also had several homes for our Governors. In those homes, many strange things have happened. Three Governors have committed suicide and, because of this, some people say the Governor's Mansion is haunted. However, one suicide was in another house, one was in St. Louis, and one was in Tennessee. None were in the present Mansion.

Another Governor and his wife died from automobile exhaust fumes while they slept but they were not sleeping in the Mansion so any story of their haunting is just silliness. However, there was one interesting story that fits in our collection of tales from Mysterious Missouri.

The New Governor's Mansion in 1872

When Governor Crittenden was in office back in 1882, tragedy struck the first family. A diphtheria epidemic swept through Middle America and many Missourians became ill. Those who were strong enough survived but many children and elderly people didn't. The Governor's nine-year-old daughter, Carrie was one who didn't.

Today, when you visit the Governor's Mansion, you can still see Carrie playing in "The Children's Fountain" near the front door. Of course, it isn't really Carrie. It's a bronze statue of her. But some say they've seen or heard the real Carrie. Some say she laughs, bangs on pipes and plays with the elevator.

The most famous "Carrie story" came exactly one hundred years after her death. Governor and Mrs. Kit Bond were having problems with the air-conditioning in 1982 and a repairman went into the attic where he found the problem. He worked up there all day and finally got everything right. When he came down, he told the staff that, if the Bonds were looking for their little girl she was up there. "You might want to mention to them that their little girl is playing around up there. She spent most of the day with me."

Of course the Bonds didn't have a little girl. So who was the nine-year-old girl playing in the attic? The repairman thought he knew. He refused to go back up there again. What do you think?

The Governor's Mansion Today

Strange Occurrences

The Joplin Spook Light

One story tells us that a miner was on his way home from work when he got lost in the woods. Worried about him, his wife grabbed a lantern and went looking. Carrying that old lantern she wandered all through the night. She went home in the morning and found that he had not yet returned. So on the second night she took her lantern and went looking for him again. The story tells us that he never made it home but she continued to look every night for the rest of her life – and after. Yes, she is supposed to be carrying that lantern through the forest even tonight.

Now, night after night people come to a road near the little town of Hornet, Missouri and wait for dark. Then, night after night a mysterious light appears and begins to move around from place to place. Sometimes the light will split into three or five smaller lights and change colors.

No one knows how long this strange thing has been going on but we do have reports and pictures from more than a hundred years ago. Some claim that the light was seen as long ago as the 1830s. Some reports claim a sighting in 1866 just after the War Between the States. The first actual documentation of a sighting was in 1881.

In 1946 the U.S. Army Corps of Engineers came from Fort Leonard Wood to study the "Hornet Light" but just couldn't find out what the thing was. They finally reported that it was a "mysterious light of unknown origin."

Photo of the Joplin Spook Light
from the early 1900s. (wikipedia)

The area is known today as the "Devil's Promenade" and is often full of carloads of people wanting to see the light for themselves. They see what many describe as a ball of light but they never know what color to expect it to be. It is different from night to night. Not everyone thinks the light looks like a ball. Some describe it as looking like a lantern traveling two or three feet off the ground.

One related phenomenon has been reported. Some witnesses claim that cows will sometimes come and stand in a circle around the light. Then the cows start making humming noises which sound like people praying.

Several people have explained that the light is caused by cars traveling down Route 66 and while they were telling this explanation, everyone sighed a sigh of relief and thought, "That explains everything. It's just some distant headlights." However, there were sightings and even pictures long before automobiles existed. Remember also that Route 66 is gone but the light is still there. Besides, if the answer was that simple, the Corps of Engineers would have figured it out. Personally, I'm glad that we don't have a good explanation. I like a little mystery in my life.

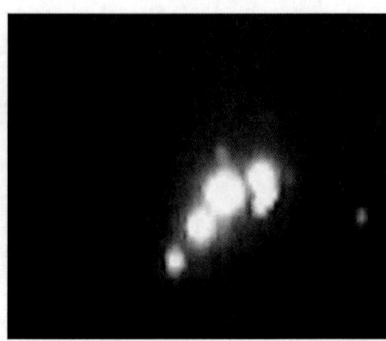

Modern Picture of the Spook Light

The Trail of Tears

Larry Baggett was a man with a mission. He didn't know that until one night he woke up at his rural home near Jerome, Missouri. He was hearing a knock at his door. He heard the same kind of knocking the next night and the next. Even though Larry woke up several nights in a row because of the knocking, his watch dog never woke up. It seems that the dog couldn't hear the knocking!

One day Larry mentioned his strange happenings to a friend who happened to be a Cherokee Indian. According to Larry the friend told him, "Well, yeah – you've built your retaining wall right across the Trail of Tears, and the spirits can't get over it, so they're just congregating around your front door.

Of course Larry didn't want to offend the Cherokee spirits so he asked his friend if he should take the wall down. His friend told him that wouldn't be necessary. "No, he said, "just build some steps so they can get over it."

Larry built the steps and what do you think? He never heard the knocking again!

Then Larry began to think about the poor Cherokee souls who were still wandering along the path of that sad and terrible journey. He decided to build a monument to them so people would never forget what the Cherokee people experienced. Soon sandstone rocks and cement were forming into arches, wells, little buildings and figures of all sorts. Then he started forming plaster statues showing old Cherokee folk tales and even a statue of himself greeting any and all visitors.

Trail of Tears Monument

For years one stone or plaster monument followed another as Baggett worked to remember the terrible event that took place on his property. More important than that was his effort to remember and honor the people who were treated so shamelessly. Soon people were swinging their cars off of Route 66 and into his drive because the monument and Larry Bagget himself had become Route 66 legends.

Larry died several years ago and his life's work is now overgrown with weeds and the monuments and statues are crumbling. It sounds rather sad doesn't it? But let's remember that we are still talking about Larry and about the experience of the Cherokee People. He became somewhat famous and the story of his Cherokee friends is still alive. So, in some ways, he was quite successful. Do you think his spirit might be traveling now with his native friends? I hope so!

The Exorcism

You may have seen the truly frightening movie, "The Exorcist." In this movie a girl was possessed by the devil and priests from Georgetown University performed an exorcism and drove the devil out of her. Well, those events really happened – sort of. You see, It wasn't a girl but a thirteen-year-old boy and the Catholic college wasn't Georgetown. It was really St. Louis University.

The events of the real story happened in a house in suburban St. Louis, the rectory of St. Francis Xavier College Church (St. Louis University), and at the Alexian Brothers Hospital in St. Louis. Both the rectory and the hospital are now gone. Only the house remains.

One detail of this story is often overlooked. It seems that the boy in the story had received a Ouija board as a gift. He was fascinated with it and was often using it and trying to contact spirits.

The events began on January 15, 1949 when the family began hearing noises in the walls and beneath the floors of the

30

boy's room. The boy said that at night, he could hear "squeaking shoes" walking around his bed.

On March 9, 1949 the priests were called to meet the boy. They found the boy sitting perfectly still on his bed but the bed was shaking violently. When the priests mentioned the Bible, the boy screamed out in pain and scrapes and welts rose up on his skin. These welts formed letters and words. When a priest asked the boy who was doing this, welts rose on the boys leg and formed a clear picture of the devil.

Two days later things got weird in another way. When the priests entered the boy's room things began to move. Everything from a tiny bottle of holy water to a large bookcase full of books moved around in the room.

On March 16 the actual exorcism began. More scratches and welts immediately appeared on the boy's skin sometimes forming words. As the weeks went by the boy would spit at the priests and scream at them in a strange high-pitched voice.

On March 21 the family agreed to move the boy to the Alexian Brothers Hospital. The hospital had a psychiatric ward where the boy could be restrained and not hurt himself. The move would be made in the wee hours of the morning so other people wouldn't be able to see what was happening to the poor child.

A friend of one of the priests told this writer that the move to the hospital was memorable. For some reason the vehicle they used did not go west toward the hospital but east toward Illinois. Then, in the middle of one of the Mississippi River bridges, something happened. The boy got loose and did things so awful and so frightening that they have never been officially reported.

They finally got him to the hospital and the ordeal continued until the day after Easter. On Monday, April 18, late at night, the boy spoke. It seemed that maybe the devil was speaking through the boy. The strange voice said, "He has to say one more word. One little word. I mean one big word. He'll never say it. I am always in him. I may not have much power always but I am in him. He'll never say that word."

Was the devil making a deal with them or just taunting them. It turns out that he chose a word in another language from a thousand years ago that the boy would never know.

At 10:45 the priest was praying over the boy. The priest was tired and worn. He had lost forty pounds during the ordeal but he continued. The boy was asleep and the priest said "Satan! Satan! I am St. Michael, and I command you Satan, and the other evil spirits to leave the body in the name of *Dominus*, immediately. Now! NOW! N-O-W!"

A few minutes later the boy woke up, looked around and said, "He's gone."

Afterwards the boy told the priests and his family that he saw a "vision" of the devil and ten of his helpers in a fierce battle with St. Michael the Archangel. During the battle the angel smiled at the boy and said *"Dominus"* which is Latin for Lord. That turned out to be the word that the devil said the boy would never say.

Most of the adults involved in this event lived full rich lives but are now gone. The identity of the boy was never revealed but researchers think they have figured out who he was. He is now in his 70s and has lived a happy life since those terrible days in 1949.

Dueling on Bloody Island

Long ago in Europe dueling was considered a way to prove who was right and who was wrong. Dueling was usually done with swords and it was thought that God would step in and make sure that the correct and truthful person would win. Actually I doubt that God bothered himself too much with a couple of grown men who were trying to stick sharp pieces of metal through each other.

At any rate, the practice continued through several centuries and involved many different weapons. The weapon of choice gradually became the pistol. The duels were conducted under a loose and changeable set of rules known as the *code duello*. The most widely recognized group of rules came from Ireland and spelled out the procedure from the moment of insult, through the duel's procedure, and to the conclusion of the duel itself.

The basic rules held that the seconds (best friends of the duelers) would write out a place and time for the parties to meet. They also chose the weapons to be used and, if pistols, they would agree on the distance between the shooters. The most important job of the seconds was to continuously attempt to settle the argument and prevent the bullets from flying.

Movies usually show the duels as a fight to the death but that was not at all true. The idea was to stand and display your bravery. Many duels ended with minor wounds or scratches and many ended with no wounds at all. In fact sometimes shots were never fired. Bloodshed could be avoided if the person who issued the challenge declared that he was satisfied.

St. Louis dueling 200 years ago usually took place on a thickly wooded sandbar called Bloody Island near the center of the Mississippi River. Residents had watched it grow out of the river in 1798. Another island in the Mississippi River near Ste. Genevieve was also used for dueling.

The most famous duel in Missouri was between the state's first two U.S. Senators. David Barton and Thomas Hart Benton were political opposites who each seem to have been trying to enhance their political reputations and careers. Politics brought the hothead Benton to duels with several other prominent St. Louisans.

What has been called "The Duel of the Governors" pitted Benjamin Brown against Thomas C. Reynolds in August of 1831. They fought over the emancipation of slaves. When the War Between the States began, Brown was elected Governor of Missouri and those favoring a Confederate government elected Reynolds as their Governor.

All of this was about honor but it's hard to see what is honorable about two men standing five or even ten paces apart and carefully pointing guns at each other. If your arm is almost three feet long, how could you miss? When they were doing all of this it was illegal in Missouri and also in Illinois. They convinced themselves that Bloody Island was right in the middle and not subject to the laws of either state. Of course they were wrong and they knew it!

So, where is Bloody Island? Can you go there today? First, remember that it's a sandbar and sandbars move. In 1837 a young army engineer , Robert E. Lee, was in St. Louis to try and control the flow of the river and keep it from eroding the "Laclede Landing" area of St. Louis. He came up with a system of dikes that forced the current out and away from St. Louis. This caused the channel to be deeper and it caused the Bloody Island sandbar to move eastward away from the city.

Now it's on the Illinois side and you can see it right under the Poplar Street Bridge. It's where all of the train tracks are today. It's a far cry from the days when hot-tempered men pretending to be gentlemen tried to shoot hot pieces of lead through each other in the name of honor!

There is a strange chapter of Missouri dueling that came several years after the shooting stopped on Bloody Island. A young hot-tempered man named William Hickok came through St. Louis and then on westward to the Springfield area. He had a wild reputation and people began to call him "Wild Bill." One day a man was giving him a hard time and Hickok invited him to step out into the Town Square and have a duel.

But this time, there were no exact rules. The two men stood and stared at each other until finally, one of them reached for his gun. Hickok could "draw" his gun out of the holster fastest so he shot and killed the other man. This became the very first of what people came to call the "quick draw" gunfight that was a feature of the old west. We will never know just how many men died in formal duels and the quick draw duels across Missouri in the 1800s but there were many of them!

Mother Returns to Help Children

We'll call her Rose Ann. She was the aunt of a lady I knew in North Missouri. That lady told me Rose Ann's story. Like most people there, her family lived on a farm and things were going very well for them. She and her husband worked hard and the farm prospered. Rose Ann was the mother of two children, a boy and a girl. She had other family members living nearby on their own farms. So life was very good.

Then Rose Ann became ill. She quickly slipped deeper and deeper into an illness that the doctors of that day didn't recognize. Within two weeks she died.

Her husband loved her dearly and he had trouble coping with the loss. He just wasn't strong enough to handle her death. Teachers at the local school noticed that the children weren't as clean and well-cared-for as usual. Neighboring farmers noticed that the fields and fencerows were not well maintained as they had always been. Something was wrong at home. It turned out to be whiskey.

The young man was trying to deal with his loss by drinking. Of course we know that alcohol is never a good solution but people who drink never realize that. Things got worse and worse.

Rose Ann's sister, Jane, lived a few miles away and they had always felt very close to each other so she was also extremely sad about this untimely death. In fact she was thinking about Rose Ann the very moment that something happened.

Jane was in her kitchen drying the dishes she had just washed when she looked toward the kitchen door to see Rose Ann standing there. "Rose Ann?" she said.

The visitor said, "The children need your help," and went away.

Jane couldn't drive the family's car so she ran through the farm field until she reached her husband. "I have to get to Rose Ann's house fast," she said. I'll tell you about it on the way."

They drove as fast as possible to Rose Ann's house and found her husband passed out in a drunken stupor. Then they found the children in their rooms – both with extremely high fevers. Carrying them to the car, they sped into the nearest town where there was a doctor.

With his help they were able to lower the children's fevers and they soon recovered. Another result of the events that day was that the father no longer felt so separated from his wife. He felt like she was there and connected with them. He wanted her to be proud of him so he worked to become a great father. It was a truly happy ending thanks to the visit of a dead Rose Ann.

Strange Times at Cape G.

Newspapers are always kept for many years at libraries and museums. They tell us about what was happening at other times in history. But – just try and find a good newspaper from Cape Girardeau or Sikeston between May 8 and May 22, 1941. People who look at those papers today will find entire sections painted over with black ink so no one call tell what stories were there. It's clear that something was happening in that area and someone doesn't want us to know just what it was.

According to the wife of a local Baptist minister, this is the story. Rev. William Huffman was called from his home to the site of a crash. Arriving there he found it wasn't a car crash or a plane crash. The craft he saw was in the shape of a saucer. He was told that there were occupants in the craft but they were dead and the officials asked if he would say a prayer for them.

When he looked into the saucer he saw that the occupants were only about four feet tall with large round eyes. They had noses and mouths but those were very small. He said that their arms were long and thin and that their hands had only three fingers each.

The authorities told him not to tell anyone what he saw but he did tell his family that very evening. Rev. Huffman told his wife that the little "men" were wearing some sort of uniform and that the saucer had all sorts of instruments inside. On the outside there were strange markings that he didn't recognize.

The minister never told anyone else about that day's events. He took the news to his grave. However, on her deathbed, Mrs. Huffman shared the news with the world. She told what had been told to her and that sent people scrambling to the libraries and museums to see what local papers might have to say about any unusual events. And, as you know, huge sections of the local papers were painted over with ink. Will we ever hear from anyone else about that strange event in 1941?

Mutilations

Near Belton, Missouri in 1978 there were two Air Force bases, a missile launch base, a Naval Air Station, and Kansas City International Airport. People in Belton were accustomed to seeing things in the sky. But, just as it was getting dark on this summer evening, August 8, several military personnel saw a UFO fly over and it stayed in the area for about 45 minutes. The military bases even tracked in on radar.

On that very same day, on the far side of the state, at Elsberry, Missouri another cow had been found mutilated. You see, there had been others. Earlier that summer six young cows were found in fields near Elsberry. Their ears, tongues, eyes, and sex organs had all been removed. There was no blood anywhere! No one could find any tracks or footprints at the scene – no evidence of any kind. Usually vultures, coyotes, and other scavengers would be all over dead animals but no scavengers would go near these cows. "Crystallized" rubbery flies were found in trees near the bodies.

Then on June 8, another farmer found a similar mutilated calf. He made a point to be vigilant the next night and that's when he saw a UFO "as big as the Moon" flying over the same field as where the calf had been found.

Eight days later. June 16, another UFO was seen flying over another farm nearby. It flew in an arc and made no sound at all. It glowed bright red. The next day another mutilated calf was found on that farm. Dead cows were found on three farms on the 17th. On the 18th bright UFOs were reported over Elsberry.

Over a period of three years these strange mutilations were found in Wentzville, Sedalia, Peculiar, Oak Grove, Blue Springs, Iberia, Dixon, and Buffalo. Three were found near Richland.

Rising Caskets

Now there could never be a case of caskets coming up out of the ground and swirling around people – or could there? Actually it did happen in 1993 and the case was well-documented in newspapers and on television. Surprisingly none of the Missourians involved were frightened. They just got busy catching the caskets so they could return them and the bodies inside back to their proper resting place.

It sounds too weird to be true, doesn't it? But, you see, in 1993 much of Missouri was under water. Terrible flooding was taking place in river valleys along the Mississippi, Missouri, Meramec, Bourbeuse, Loutre, and Gasconade Rivers. As more and more water soaked into the ground, the ground became softer and softer until it was nothing much more than soft mud.

Trapped under the ground were big boxes with dead bodies and lots of air. (caskets) If something is underwater and filled with air it will try to rise to the top of the water. That's just what the caskets did. Up through the soft mud and on to the surface.

Pop, pop, pop, the caskets sprang up and the local people got out in their boats and tried to get ropes on them before they swirled away in the current of the rivers. Later when the water went down and things got back to normal, people did their best to get each coffin back to its proper place. So, when people tell you that the dead can't rise from their graves, you just tell them that in 1993 they sure did!

Strange People

From Masada to Missouri?

Way back in the year 72 – that's right almost 2000 years ago – the Romans had attacked Israel and had destroyed the great Temple just as Jesus had predicted they would. They were determined to punish and maybe even destroy the people of Israel. Some of those people fled to a fortress in the desert called Masada.

Masada was high on the top of a mountain where it seemed no army could attack. It was big enough to have gardens and livestock. It even had its own secret water supply way out there in the desert. But the Romans were patient. It took a long time but they finally built a gigantic ramp up the side of the mountain and sent their armies to overrun the fortress and kill the people or take them as slaves.

The Israelites refused to be taken prisoner or to be killed by the Romans so they committed mass suicide just before the Romans swarmed over the walls. We know all of this because the historian, Josephus, wrote all about it. But he also wrote something else about that day.

According to Josephus, some of the Israelites called the Sicarii, escaped at the last minute and got away. Being a little different from other Jews, this Sicarii group always wore their hair in long braids. Otherwise they were typical people for their time and place. At any rate, this Sicarii Tribe was lost to history.

Several years ago, at a meeting in Columbia, Missouri, I was talking with two Chiefs of the Northern Cherokee Nation and they told me of an important story from their people's past. According to the Cherokee legend, their people did not always live in North America. They claim to have come from far away across the Great Water.

The Northern Cherokee say that their people were trapped by a much larger army and were sure to die when someone came up with a plan to escape. Their people sneaked out of their homes and journeyed across a huge desert and then across the Great Water to arrive in America. All this time, they say, they were being chased by a group of their enemies. Across the desert and across the ocean they fled while their enemies pursued them.

Some of these Northern Cherokee even think that the Roman pursuers who chased them made it to America also and the soldiers eventually married Indian wives and formed the nation known today as the Chickasaw. The Chickasaw and the Cherokee have always been traditional enemies. The Chickasaw people don't agree with the Cherokee story at all but you wouldn't expect them to.

What do you think? Could the Northern Cherokee story be true? There are some reasons to think it might be. For instance the people who fled the Masada were called the Sicarii which sounds a lot like Cherokee. And you know that words and the way we pronounce them change over the years.

We know that most Israelites didn't braid their hair but the Sicarii did. Most Indians don't braid their hair but the Cherokee do. The Jews had an alphabet and could write. The Cherokee were the only Indians with an alphabet and writing.

There's one more important thing. At an Indian burial mound in Bat Creek, Tennessee a stone was found. It had carvings that radio-carbon dating shows us are from about 2000 years ago. Some anthropologists tell us that the carvings are an early form of Hebrew writing. Other anthropologists tell us that the carvings are an early form of Cherokee writing. Maybe they are both! Maybe early Hebrew writing and early Cherokee writing are the same thing!

The Bat Creek Stone

Now I've included this story in a section of the book called "Strange People" and there is absolutely nothing strange about the Northern Cherokee people. But wouldn't it be strange if someone did prove that this Lost Tribe of Israel was actually our own Northern Cherokee tribe in Missouri?

A Mad Doctor

Dr. Joseph Nash McDowell was a great medical doctor and teacher in St. Louis. He is remembered for starting a medical college there to train new doctors. Like him, however, the college was a little strange. This odd looking building was built like a fort and had a tower with cannons sticking out of portholes in the tower. One cannon was said to be from the pirate ship of Jean Lafitte.

Dr. McDowell wore an armor breastplate to keep anyone from killing him and he kept muskets at the school to be handed out in case anyone would want to attack the school. Someone who knew him said he had "an erratic temperament that approached insanity."

During the War Between the States the Union army seized the school and used it as a prison. After the war Dr. McDowell re-opened his medical school but at a different location.

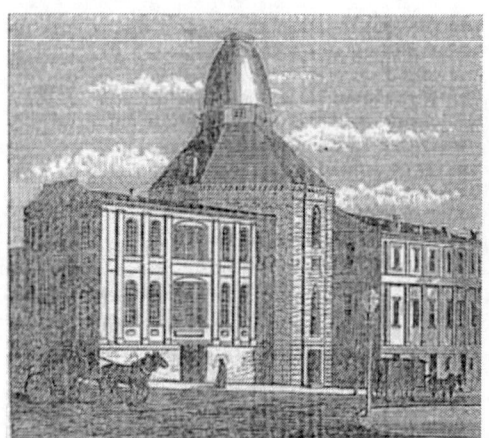

The McDowell Medical College

Dr. McDowell had a museum inside his medical college. The museum had lots of exotic animals including over 3000 birds. There were also minerals, fossils, and antiques. He charged 25 cents for admission but allowed ministers and doctors to enter for free. He also gave medical treatment to poor people for free. What a nice guy! He also hated Catholics, immigrants, and African-Americans. What a rotten guy!

Now if you ran a medical school, you would need cadavers wouldn't you? Cadavers are the dead bodies of people and young medical students can cut them open to look inside and see what our organs are like. So where do you suppose Dr. McDowell got his cadavers? He was a body snatcher!

That's right – The doctor would take his students out for night raids on the local cemeteries. The grave robbers would then bring the bodies back to school for the next week's lessons. If your teacher ever asks you to be a grave robber, tell him or her that you don't feel like it.

Some residents were horrified at the rumors of what was going on at the college. Mobs would gather and attack the school. One time the good doctor went to his museum and got a bear. Then he had his bear attack the crowd! My doctor has never done that!

Dr. McDowell didn't always live in St. Louis. He also took his weirdness to Hannibal. There he did secret autopsies and experiments on dead bodies. Do you remember the stories of Mark Twain like The Adventures of Tom Sawyer? Twain describes the grave robbing by Muff Potter and Injun Joe for "young Dr. Robinson." The young Doctor was modeled after our Dr. McDowell who lived in Hannibal at that time and owned what is now called Mark Twain Cave.

And remember, I said that he did secret autopsies and experiments on dead bodies. Two of those bodies were his own children. When they died he didn't bury them. He wrapped them up and hung them from the ceiling of the cave. No wonder Mark Twain thought it was a spooky place!

Ouija Board Lady

Pearl Lenore Curran was a normal girl but she never did like school. She made pretty crummy grades and eventually just dropped out. She did like music and learned how to play a few instruments to go along with a very nice singing voice.

Eventually Pearl got married and lived with her husband in St. Louis. Everything was pretty normal in her life until July 8, 1913 when she and two friends tried to use a ouija board. When Pearl held the indicator it spelled the message, "Many moons ago I lived. Again I come. Patience Worth my name." Then this lady, Patience Worth, went on to say, "Wait, I would speak with thee. If thou shalt live, then so shall I. I make my bread at thy hearth. Good friends, let us be merrie. The time for work is past. Let the tabby drowse and blink her wisdom to the firelog."

The mysterious Patience Worth then went on to dictate stories to Pearl Curran. The result was several books and many poems. And they were good ones. Pearl was a school dropout who never liked writing but with her Ouija board she created literary works described by the New York Times as "tipped with the flame of genius."

Eventually Patience Worth said that she lived from 1649 to 1694 and she came from rural England to America on a three-masted sailing ship. She lived in America for years and was eventually killed by Indians.

All of her books, poems and descriptions have been checked over by historians and experts and all of them seem to be accurate. How could this fairly uneducated woman in St. Louis know and be able to write about life in another place and hundreds of years earlier? This is truly a wonderful mystery to think about!

General Nathaniel Lyon

There is an old saying that "The winners write the history books." This may be why some consider General Nathaniel Lyon to be a hero. This writer considers him to be something closer to a devil. He was at least weird beyond words. Even before he came to Missouri he had led his soldiers in a terrible massacre of men, women, and children.

It seems that when the young officer, Nathaniel Lyon, was stationed in California there was a law that anyone not working at another job could be forced to work in the mines and ranches. Some folks decided that since Indians didn't work in stores and banks and what others might call a job, then they could take the Indians and force them to work on the ranches. Of course this is slavery and, to make it worse, some of the ranchers were taking only the women to their ranches.

One day a rancher took a chief's beautiful wife to live at his ranch. The Indians attacked the ranch and rescued the woman. Then Nathaniel Lyon led his troops into action against the Indians to punish them. When he found the entire tribe camped on an island he made a plan. He sent some of his men to attack from the front while most of his men sneaked around to attack from behind. Surprising the Indians, he easily killed all of them except for a very few who escaped to tell the story.

Then everyone found out that Lyon had attacked the wrong tribe of Indians. With this scandal, he was transferred back east and stationed at Jefferson Barracks in St. Louis. The problem developed when his commander got into a scandal of his own and had to be transferred away from St. Louis. This left Lyon in charge of the largest military unit west of the Mississippi.

As it began to look like there might be a war between the states, Lyon became obsessed with people who had ideas different than his. Then, one day, a group of southern sympathizers met in a rally in St. Louis. Lyon felt that he had to know what was going on so, instead of sending a spy, he disguised himself and went out to the meeting.

In his disguise he was supposed to be an old woman so he did wear a dress but he still had a problem because he had a big bushy black beard. Lyon put a scarf across the beard but it's hard to imagine that he fooled many people. The next day he sent his soldiers out to round up the people attending the meeting and brought them back to St. Louis even though they had broken no laws.

On the way back people began to yell "Boo" at the soldiers and even spit at them. Lyon told his men to start shooting at the crowd. It didn't seem to matter to him that many of the people in the crowd were just watching. The crowd even included some other Generals and their families who had to duck for cover.

The next day people were still very angry so he ordered his troops to shoot the protesters again. This two-day event has come to be known as the "St. Louis Massacre." When war finally did break out some leaders in Missouri had a plan to keep Missourians from fighting and just remain neutral. Nathaniel Lyon said that he would rather see, "every man, woman, and child in the state dead and buried." Missouri eventually saw 1106 battles and skirmishes and, more than any other person, Lyon was responsible for those.

After the war was underway Lyon continued to do strange things. Missouri never did leave the Union or join the South but Lyon still loaded his troops on riverboats and took over Jefferson City. During a battle Lyon was known to stop and slather mustard on big slices of bread. He would then eat his mustard sandwiches while the bullets flew. He was a strange man!

Finally (for him) a large group of southern soldiers were joined by some northern soldiers to stop Lyon who many considered to have lost his mind. At the Battle of Wilson's Creek Lyon was killed and his body was hidden so the Southerners wouldn't know they had killed a Union General. Eventually the Union troops were able to get his body away and into Springfield.

In Springfield they buried him in Mrs. Phelps's rose garden until the Southern army left. Then, a few days later, they dug him up (ughh!) and put him on a slow train to Washington, D.C. This guy was doing weird things even after his death!

Gen. Nathaniel Lyon
(wikipedia)

So, the next time you see Lyon, Missouri on the map or a statue of General Lyon in the park, or a portrait hanging in your library, remember that his side needed heroes. This time they picked a really strange one, didn't they?

Alf Bolin

There's good and bad in everyone – right? Well, in southern Missouri the people will say, "There weren't nuthin' good about Alf Bolin." He was lower than a snake in the rocks around Forsyth, Missouri.

Not much is known about Alf until the Civil War began. Then we know that he organized a gang of somewhere between twenty and fifty men who terrorized south Missouri. He claimed to be fighting for the Confederacy but it's probably closer to the truth to say that he was fighting against authority. He was just taking advantage of the fact that most of the able-bodied men were away from home and at the war.

There was a place that came to be called Bolin's Rocks or Murder Rocks. There the gang ambushed people passing on the road below. He let nothing stop him. No one knows how many people he killed during his time along the Fox Creek but at least fourteen murders of old men, children, and women have been documented. He also killed at least two soldiers.

Finally the Union army figured out a way to stop him. A soldier named Zach Thomas went to the home of the Foster family. Mr. Foster was a southern sympathizer and was a prisoner of war. Foster was promised a release if his family would help with the plan to get Alf Bolin. The union soldier, Thomas, was disguised as a Confederate soldier. Thomas pretended to be sick as he stayed for several days hoping that Alf Bolin would appear.

Finally Bolin did come to the house and was hacked with a plowshare by the soldier. They took the body into another room only to discover that he was not dead. So they killed him again. Bolin's life ended at age 21.

When they took the body to Forsyth a street celebration began. The good citizens decapitated Bolin and put the head on a pole in the center of Ozark, Missouri. This was on May 15, 1863. Since that time, people wanting to get married or looking for a good day to celebrate can choose to do so on what has been called Alf Bolin Day. May 15 is a charmed and lucky day in the Forsyth area!

There is one last part to this story. Since the gang was so active and pulled so many robberies, there is a story of loot hidden and marked with the skull of a horse. But only Bolin knew just where to look. Now Treasure hunters continue to scour the area along Route JJ ten miles south of Forsyth near Gobbler's Knob. If someone finds that treasure it will be a good thing. Otherwise, there weren't nuthin' good about Alf Bolin.

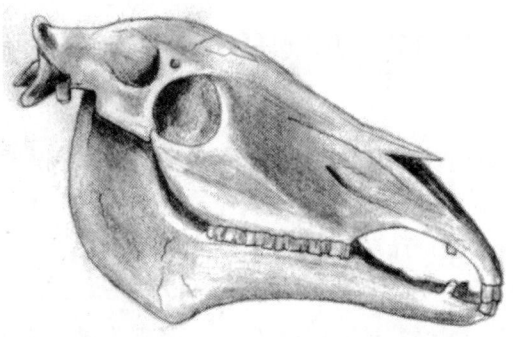

Look for the Horse's Skull

Chief White Hair

White Hair was one of the Principal Chiefs of the great Osage Nation. And he was a good one. But I want to tell you a story of powerful medicine. The story of how White Hair got his name.

When the young Osage warrior was called upon by his tribe to fight a battle, he was ready. This was before the Louisiana Purchase so Missouri was still occupied by the British. During the battle the young brave pounced upon a British officer wearing a bright red uniform and a white powdered wig. Holding the officer down, the brave drew his knife and prepared to scalp the soldier.

The officer came to his senses in time to see the Indian holding his hair and preparing to cut it off. He screamed and ran away leaving the young brave with a puzzled look on his face and holding the white man's scalp (the wig) in his left hand.

The other braves saw what had happened and declared that wig to be powerful medicine. It gave the Englishman another life and it gave the warrior a scalp for his lodge pole. With it, everyone got what they wanted. The white "scalp" became the most wonderful thing in the tribe and its owner had great prestige.

By the time William Clark met White Hair, the chief was very old and when he died he left the scalp to his son. The son was then called Young White Hair and this son helped the people at Fort Osage in Jackson County. I wish I had a picture of the look on the warrior's face when the soldier ran away leaving his scalp behind!

Missouri Governors

Wouldn't you like to be the Governor of Missouri some day? Don't answer that question too quickly. You know there have been some strange and tragic things connected to our governors and to the Governor's Mansion.

Our very first Governor was not elected but appointed by The President. When The Territory of Louisiana was established with St. Louis as the seat of government, James Wilkinson was named the first Governor. It turned out that Wilkinson was a close friend of the notorious spy, Benedict Arnold and that Wilkinson himself was a double agent (spy) for the Spanish.

Wilkinson plotted with another notorious traitor, Aaron Burr, to raise an army in Missouri and separate this territory from the United States and then attack and rule Mexico. So Missouri and Mexico and everything in between would be one gigantic country ruled by Burr and Wilkinson. On March 3, 1807, our Governor Wilkinson was branded a traitor and a spy and expelled from his office.

Next, Thomas Jefferson chose his friend, Meriwether Lewis for the job. Lewis had done such a wonderful job on the Lewis and Clark Expedition but as soon as he became Governor things started going bad.

He just couldn't get anything done. He created problems with the Indians in Missouri. He started gambling and drinking whiskey. Jefferson was getting very worried about him and told him to come back to Washington for a visit. On the way back, September 3, 1809, he stopped for the night at Grinder's Stand,

Tennessee. That night he was shot to death. Some say he shot himself.

Then there was poor old Governor Boggs. He turned out to be in charge when the Honey War (against Iowa) and the Mormon War broke out. He is the one who said that all Mormons should be chased out or killed and he didn't care which. History would always think of him as silly because of the Honey War and awful because of the Mormon War.

Abraham Williams was a good Governor and I only mention him here because he was unusual in one way. He had just one leg. He will be remembered for that but also for the good work he did in the State Senate and back at his home in Boone County.

In 1844 Governor Thomas Reynolds committed suicide in the Governor's Mansion. He shot himself with a handgun. Remember, this was 28 years before our present Governor's Mansion was built.

In 1887 another man named Thomas Reynolds committed suicide. This man had been the Confederate Governor of Missouri during the War Between the States. His wife's nightgown had caught fire at the fireplace and she died from her burns. He felt so bad that he thought he couldn't get over it so while he was in a tall building in St. Louis, he jumped down an elevator shaft.

The strangest of all may have been the Governor who could win elections even though he was dead. On October 16, 2000 the airplane of former Governor, Mel Carnahan crashed killing everyone aboard. At the time he was running for a seat in the U.S. Senate and trailing badly in the polls. It looked as if there was no way he could win. Then, after he was dead, the people of Missouri tried to show their sympathy by electing him to that high office!   But, people around the country laughed at Missouri for electing a dead man to office.

The Good Samaritan

I really don't want to tell too much about this lady because she still has family members living in Missouri and there is no need to make them feel worse than they already do. So I won't use the lady's real name. People called her "The Good Samaritan" because of all the great ways that she helped people.

This lady lived in the rural counties of East Central Missouri and she always looked for opportunities to help people. She really liked people and she really liked her farm. The one thing she didn't like were the rats that got into her corn and other grains. She learned how to poison those rats with arsenic.

From time to time some child would get sick and the parents would spend long days and nights with the poor child as it got sicker and sicker. Everyone seemed to know that the child was going to die but the parents would stand by and do everything they could all day and all night hoping for a miracle. Then our sweet old lady would show up and bring a nice meal for everyone. Next she would shoo the parents out the door to go and see a movie or do what ever they wanted to relax for just one night.

When they returned home they would thank the lady and call her a saint or a Good Samaritan. She would return home and the child would die the next day or so. People would always say things like, "It's so sad but I sure am glad that the nice lady came by and gave the parents a break."

As time went by people began to grow suspicious and they started looking a little deeper into the events around the area. In 1928 the lady went to Eureka to do some shopping and she was arrested there. She was later tried and sentenced to serve the rest of her life in prison for killing a man with rat poison.

They didn't try her for every death because it would just be a waste of the court's time and money. However they think that she killed as many as seventeen men and children with arsenic in those wonderful meals she cooked.

So off to prison she went and spent the rest of her life there. In prison people are assigned jobs to do and the Good Samaritan was assigned her duties also. She spent the rest of her life cooking delicious meals for the other prisoners. That's right, the lady who poisoned people with her food was told to spend years preparing food for even more people!

More Rats!

The *Audrain County Repubican* newspaper reported in 1876 that Mr. David Crockett had killed 341 rats in his corn cribs. That's very interesting but why did he wait so long. How could he let 341 rats live in his harvested corn?

Baldknobbers

There was a time before, during and after the War Between the States that Missouri was a pretty lawless place. Instead of the "Show-Me State" many people called this the "Outlaw State." In far southwest Missouri a group of leaders got together and decided that the local sheriffs were no match for the great number of outlaws so they decided to help.

Starting with good intentions and led by a man named Nat Kinney, they formed secret squads of horsemen who could move fast and react quickly every time there was trouble. People who do this have to be "vigilant" which means they have to always be on the lookout for trouble. So folks call them "vigilantes."

The sheriffs had to take time and do everything by the law. They had to swear in a posse, be polite to everyone as they chased the bad guys, and then try not to hurt the bad guys but bring them back to the county seat for a trial. These new vigilantes didn't mess with any of that. They just chased the bad guys down and punished them. Sometimes they used a whip, sometimes they used a gun, and sometimes they would hang the bad guys from a tree. Sometimes they made mistakes and punished the wrong people.

These vigilantes had to operate in secret so they wouldn't have to worry about answering for their deeds. They wore uniforms including masks with horns so they could all look just alike and also so they could scare everyone.

Baldknobbers with horned masks waiting in ambush

In the Ozarks a hill is often called a "knob" and a hill with no trees on the top is called a "bald knob." The vigilantes liked to have their meetings on a bald knob because no one could sneak up on them and see who they were or what they were doing. Because of this, they called themselves the Baldknobbers.

As time went by, more and more people wanted to join the group and the group became larger and more powerful and more feared than ever before. Some of the new people joining were doing it for the wrong reasons and they just liked being powerful or cruel. Soon everyone in the Ozarks was afraid of the Baldknobbers. They became what today we would call domestic terrorists.

As they did terrible and even more terrible things, some of the good men involved began to quit and they told who the leaders were. On May 10, 1889 three of the leaders who had been caught were tried for their crimes and hanged in the town of Forsyth. The main leader, Nat Kinney, had already been tried and hanged so this was just about the end of the reign of terror. Now the Baldknobbers don't exist anywhere except in stories and plays.

Valentine Taplry

To read today's history books you would think that everyone was overjoyed with the election of Abraham Lincoln. That just wasn't true. In fact, he didn't win one single county in Missouri! For many reasons people were concerned about him winning. No one was more concerned than a man in Pike County named Valentine Taplry.

Mr. Taplry made a promise that if Lincoln won the election, he would never shave again. Of course Lincoln won but do you think Mr. Taplry kept his promise? Yes he did.

On November 6, 1860 Taplry shaved like he did every morning, got dressed and went off to vote. Then came the big news that Lincoln had won and Talpry never shaved again for the rest of his life. His beard eventually grew to be over 12 ½ feet long! That's almost twice as long as it is in the picture. When Valentine Taplry said something, he really meant it.

Valentine Taplry

Bob Berdella

Most people around Kansas City had no idea who Bob Berdella was but they may have visited his store. He owned a little business named Bob's Bizarre Bazaar. It was a place where you could buy all sorts of strange, occult, and spooky things that other stores wouldn't sell. I actually like the name of Bob's place because "bizarre" means strange and "bazaar" is a marketplace for buying all kinds of things. It truly was a bizarre bazaar!

During his school years and in college he made excellent grades. Bob had been in trouble with the police a few times because of illegal drug use when he was a college student. But all in all he wasn't such a bad guy – at least that's what people thought. Before he started his Bizarre Bazaar he worked as a chef at some of the city's best restaurants and became moderately famous.

One night in early 1988 he had a few beers at a Kansas City bar and was too drunk to drive home. Some folks at the bar agreed to drop him off. On the way he told them all sorts of wild stories about how he captured and killed young men. Of course they knew he was just talking. Sometimes drunks tell "whoppers" and people just laugh at the lies.

Then on April 2 a young man wearing a dog collar jumped from the second story window of Bob's house and escaped. The young man ran to a neighbor's house and the police were called.

The court didn't have any trouble convicting Bob and sending him off to prison because, as he tortured each man, he kept a diary and described everything that happened. He also like to take pictures and had plenty of those.

Bob explained to everyone that he really was a nice guy. Sometimes when he tortured a person he would give them antibiotics so they wouldn't get sick. That's a nice thing to do for someone – right?

The Mummy of Mount Olive

Let's look back to 1924 when a truck farmer named Joseph Marconnot died in his home town of Carondelet, Missouri. Joseph had a strong desire to be remembered after his death so he had made plans for his body when the time came. According to his wishes, he was buried in the manner of the Pharaoh, King Tutankhamun.

Just a little over two years before Joseph died King Tut's tomb had been discovered and opened in Egypt and everyone across the world was still terribly excited about it. Probably because of this, Joseph stipulated in his will that he should be embalmed like an Egyptian Pharaoh. Of course he would need to be dressed in the highest style of his day so he ordered that his embalmed body should be dressed in a tuxedo.

Also according to his wishes he was placed in a beautiful new mausoleum at the Mount Olive Cemetery and the mausoleum was to have a glass door so people could stop by and admire the Pharaoh Farmer. The neat thing is that, over the years, lots of people did come by to check him out. He became a popular attraction just the way he had planned.

But other people always think they know what's good for us don't they? One day some people started worrying about vandalism and other things so they decided to replace the plate glass door with one made of stainless steel. Now, when you visit old Joe, you can no longer see the mummified man – just a plain old everyday door.

The Marconnot Mummy's Marvelous Mausoleum

Another Mummy Behind Glass

Who would ever think that there could have been another mummy displayed behind glass for the world to admire? Well there was one but this one wasn't there of his own choosing.

On Halloween day in 1912 the St. Louis Post-Dispatch newspaper reported that the unclaimed body of a man had been standing in the window of a St. Louis mortuary for 27 years. They were displaying him to demonstrate the skill of their embalming.

Crime and Punishment

Sometimes it's easy to think that things have always been pretty much the same as they are today. That may be true for some things but, thank Goodness, some things have changed!

Whipping with a leather whip had been the regular punishment for soldiers and sailors for thousands of years and many other people practiced it also. But in 1804 the pillory and whipping post were established as the official forms of punishment in the Territory of Missouri. The whipping post was a tall pole that held a person in place while being lashed with a leather bull whip. The pillory held a person's head and wrists while they endured humiliation or physical pain. People seemed to enjoy going by the pillory and throwing rotten vegetables and other things in the criminals' faces. Some folks would get a little closer and spit in their eyes. Remember their hands were held in the pillory so they couldn't wipe the stuff out of their eyes and faces. So both pain and humiliation were important parts of the pillory and the whipping post.

Pillories for Men and Women

In 1822 the state decided to build a new courthouse for St. Louis. It's that beautiful building with the green dome in front of the Arch. That is the exact spot where the whipping post was. So they took the whipping post down but didn't replace it. In 1826 the state outlawed the use of whipping posts and pillories in Missouri.

There have been many times in history when a person felt the need to break a law. For instance, we are not supposed to kill other people but if someone is hurting a man's children, the man will often kill in order to protect his kids. Maybe it was something like that that happened in our next example.

I don't know exactly what happened down in Pulaski County in 1833 but a man, Archibald McDonald, was convicted for shooting and injuring another man in a gun fight. Mr. McDonald was sentenced to serve "one minute" in the county jail!

In 1864 the Civil War Bushwhacker known as Bloody Bill Anderson wasn't captured but he was shot in Ray County. First his head was put on a pole. Then his body dragged through the streets of Richmond, MO. Later some folks claimed that it wasn't Anderson who was ambushed that day.

Another unusual event happened in January of that year. The famous Shakespearian actor, John Wilkes Booth was performing in a play in St. Louis that month. When people applauded him, they could not have known that he would soon be in Washington, D.C. to kill President Lincoln.

Barry County had an interesting situation in 1878 when a prisoner couldn't come up with the money to post bail. (get out of jail until his trial)   He got out by leaving his wooden leg with the court.   They figured that he wouldn't want to go far without it and couldn't go far if he tried.

News reached Missouri in 1875 that Mark Twain was in trouble. When a boy stole his umbrella he offered a $205.00 reward. $5.00 was for the umbrella and $200.00 for "the boy's remains."   "The boy's remains?"   Was he really that angry about an umbrella?   Of course not – he was joking – but it sounded so bad that people were upset with him.

Then Twain was arrested when a corpse turned up at his home along with a note saying that it was the boy's remains and claiming the reward. It turned out that some jokers at a local medical college had sent a corpse to get Mark Twain in trouble. Very funny!

In may of 1936 a prisoner was brought from the state penitentiary to testify in a trial at Centerville. When he was taken from the sheriff's car six pretty young women were waiting and each gave him a warm kiss. The prisoner was Robert Camden and was known in south Missouri as the Robin Hood of Reynolds County and also as the Scourge of the Ozarks. He became so popular because he acted a little like Robin Hood while he was hiding in the forest. While hiding from the law Camden didn't want armed men in the woods so he left notes stating that hunters would be shot on sight.

So local people stopped hunting and fishing became very popular that year!   He also promised that he would do the hunting and that no one would lack for meat on their tables so he kept them supplied with venison and turkey. From time to time every house in the area would find venison or turkey at their door and it never cost them anything. They didn't even have to go hunting for it.

I can't tell you about all the things Ken McElroy did. I don't even want to think about it. He was like a bully who bullied everyone around Skidmore, Missouri. Every man, woman, and child in that part of the country were afraid of him. Finally bullies reach a point where people just can't stand it any more and they fight back.

In 1981, McElroy came out of a meeting in Skidmore to find a large crowd of people waiting for him. He shouted an insult to them and started toward his car. But then he was shot to death with at least two different kinds of rifles. The strange thing is that with at least 46 people there, no one saw anything! The bully is gone and no one was punished for the crime.

An even stranger case may have taken place in the courthouse in Union, Missouri in 1950. A very old man named Dalton came to court and confessed to all of his crimes from years ago. He said back then his name was Jesse James and that he hadn't been shot back in St. Joseph. It was just part of a plan so he could get away and live in peace.

A man named Rudy Turilli, (from Meramec Caverns) brought Dalton to live in a cabin at the cave. He was there waving and talking with people for a while before he finally died. It was a good stunt but nothing more.

Strange Heroes

When this writer was a boy, there was a TV show about a western hero named Wyatt Earp. The theme song said,

"Wyatt Earp, Wyatt Earp,
Brave, courageous, and bold.
Long live his fame and long live his glory,
And long may his story be told."

I thought he was a great man for sure. Then I got a job which sent me out to Dodge City, Kansas from time to time. There I found a larger-than-life bronze statue of Wyatt Earp right there in the historic part of town. What a guy!

At that time I didn't even know that Wyatt Earp had lived in Missouri. I did know some relatives of his from my home town but I kind of wondered how they got there. Well, of course, they were there because the Earp family had been in Missouri where they were very well known. Wyatt's father had a position of power in South Missouri and the teenaged Wyatt sometimes helped his dad. Some would say that Wyatt was a bully. Some would say that both he and his father were bullies.

I think the first time that Wyatt really got into serious trouble was when he was hired as a tax collector. His job was to go around and collect a certain amount from every family and every individual. This tax money was to support the local schools. However, Wyatt was taken to court by those schools because he kept the money instead of turning it in where it belonged.

Wyatt Earp

In 1871 Wyatt and two other men were each charged with stealing two horses. Nine days later a Deputy US Marshall arrested Earp for the theft. Just a few days after that, James Cromwell filed a lawsuit against Wyatt Earp in Barton County claiming that Earp had kept money that was owed to Cromwell. In other words, he stole the money from him.

About two months later he was still in the Barton County Jail waiting for his trial. He dug and climbed through the roof of the jail and ran away from Missouri never to come back.

Another famous western lawman didn't start out that way. William Hickock was known by most as Wild Bill. It was because of his wild behavior. He had seen the dueling that took place on Bloody Island in St. Louis and he kind of liked the idea. However, he invented a little different way to do it.

Bill was in Springfield in the summer of 1865 and ran into a man he never liked. Davis Tutt was there with some of his friends and they were all drinking whiskey at a saloon on the Springfield Square. They got into an argument and Wild Bill challenged Tutt to a duel. This time however, he said they should just step into the street and see who could pull (draw) their guns out of the holster and shoot the fastest. Hickok gave Tutt several chances to change his mind but Tutt kept teasing Hickock until he seemed to have no choice. A few minutes later Tutt lay dead and the quick-draw western-style gunfight was invented.

Of course it was against the law and Wild Bill left Missouri immediately after that gunfight but we know that he returned. There are records of him serving as an umpire for professional baseball in Kansas City. That 1866 team was the K.C. Antelopes. And, yes, he did wear both six guns while calling balls and strikes. There were probably fewer arguments that way.

Francis Tumblety

Jack the Ripper was a terrible man who lived in London, England for a time and is now known as the first modern serial killer. He called himself the "ripper" because he butchered his victims and took parts of them for souvenirs. One man named Francis Tumblety, a visitor to London, was arrested for another crime but then "skipped" the country and ran to France. The English thought for a while that he was dead. But, actually, he had come back home to Missouri. When he left England, the murders stopped.

In St. Louis Tumblety was said to be a wonderful person. At least, <u>he</u> said that he was. Everyone else seemed to think he was awful. He made and wore ridiculous uniforms even though he had never been in the military. He said that he was a medical doctor even though he had no medical training at all. He made his living by selling fake medicines that never helped people but sometimes hurt them. He spent his whole life lying and cheating people – and maybe sometimes killing them.

Francis Tumblety

Fast Eddie

One day in 2012 the quiet town of Ozark, Missouri was surprised when a huge collection of many kinds of police officers converged on the home of Edward Maher. They were surprised that this quiet family man who didn't seem to be especially wealthy was really a man known in England as Fast Eddie. Years before he had stolen $1.5 million from an armored car in London.

Fast Eddie came to America and somehow blew all of the money. He and his family began moving from state to state and finally found Ozark, MO. Ozark is the fastest-growing city in the state so it was easy for a new family to fit in and not be noticed. Then Eddie's wife won $100,000 in the Missouri Lottery. It's hard to hide when things like that happen but they did. Soon, however, they blew all of that money too.

When Fast Eddie was arrested he was working as a cable guy and his wife was working as a cleaning lady. The funny thing is that Eddie and his son had told several people about being armored car robbers from England and no one believed them. That's too bad because there was a huge reward for anyone who could help the police find them!

Strange Places

Molly Crenshaw's Grave

This is two stories about one sad woman. As the first story is told, Molly Crenshaw was a Jamaican woman brought to Missouri as a slave. After the Civil War she lived by herself in a small cabin in the woods in St. Charles County. She practiced the black art of voodoo and would sometimes be asked to do magical favors for her neighbors and they would pay her for her help.

Then, during one particularly cold and miserable winter, the neighbors began to talk and decided that Molly Crenshaw must have done something to the weather – It just wasn't normal for things to be this cold. The more they talked, the more angry they became. Then they went after Molly.

She stood her ground and refused to go along with their wild stories and told the mob that she would place a curse on any of them who bothered her any more. That made them even more angry and finally they attacked her. The story tells us that they killed poor Molly Crenshaw and cut her into pieces so she couldn't work any dark magic from her grave.

They buried the parts of the body in different places in the woods and went away thinking everything was settled. But now, the story says, each year the parts are managing to draw themselves closer and closer together. It's only a matter of time before they are all re-joined.

It's a common thing now for high school students in the area to go out looking for Molly's grave. The tombstone is gone but they all know just about where the grave is. They sometimes shout that they are not afraid of Molly and dare her to do anything to them. The spooky thing is that they often report getting lost after that or not being able to start their cars, or getting sick there in the woods.

So, how much of this is true. Well, certainly some of it is. There was a Molly Crenshaw who lived there close to where Francis Howell High School is today. However, she did spell her name "Molley." She seems to have been a sad lady who, about a hundred years ago became deaf and then committed suicide. Each year many students do go traipsing through the woods and into old cemeteries looking for the grave. And, yes, there have been cases of sickness, headaches, and automobile problems afterwards.

Molly's family removed the tombstone from the grave sometime in the 1970s because of problems with teenagers having parties and being disrespectful in the cemetery. A friend of the family now hides the tombstone in his garage because of vandalism to the stone. Today the St. Charles area has things like the "Molly Crenshaw Haunted Woods" events around Halloween. And bored teenagers continue to wander through the woods twisting their ankles and challenging fate.

Henges

I'll bet you know all about Stonehenge. It's a strange, wonderful, mysterious, and inspiring place on the Salisbury Plain in England. A "henge" is a special circle and the famous one is made of stone. There is another one nearby made of wood and called "Woodhenge." But, did you know that Missouri has it's own henge? Well, that's not exactly correct. We have three henges!

One henge is made of beautiful stone and is in Rolla on the campus of the Missouri University of Science and Technology. It was made by some of the engineering students who were learning how to cut stone using pressurized water.

Stonehenge at Rolla

Another Missouri henge is also made of stone. It is the private project of a man who just wanted to have a Stonehenge at his farm. He did a good job and it's really pretty cool! It's on the property of Steve and Alice Wagoner. They call it "The Circle" but it is a set of twelve stones placed according to the position of the sun at the summer solstice and they form a henge. The stones are as large as seven tons and they really do resemble England's Stonehenge.

"The Circle" at Patton
Photo courtesy of Rural Missouri Magazine

73

A third henge is a little hard to find. You almost have to go on the Katy Trail to find it. It's really different from the others. It's called "Boathenge" and it's made of old speedboats standing in a partial circle near Easley, Missouri just west of Columbia.

Boathenge at Easley

Promoters explain that these boats with their noses buried and their tails erect (and visa versa) just appeared on the Spring Solstice by either springing up from the ground or dropping from the sky. They aren't sure and their story doesn't matter a whole lot, does it? After all they're just some guys having fun with us.

Pete Kibble's Foot

Pete Kibble's foot is buried up in Milan, Missouri. Pete was a local guy who lost his foot in a railroad accident. He had the foot buried in Oakwood Cemetery, under a marker that reads, "Pete Kibble's Foot 1917." He did that so he would have a grave avaiable and someday, when the rest of him died, he could be reuinted with his foot. But then Pete had a change of heart and went out to the wild west never to return. As a result, there remains in Milan's Oakwood Cemetery a grave clearly marked as Pete Kibble's Foot. If you travel the world, how many things like that will you see?

Queen of the Gypsies

When was the last time that you saw a swarm of Gypsies? When was the last time that you saw even one Gypsy? Well, I'm pretty sure that you've seen them but just didn't know it. You see, in the warm months they're all around us. In cold months they mostly stay at home.

Most people don't know they've been talking or doing business with Gypsies until they realize they've been "Gypped." That's right, the word "Gypped" which means "ripped off" or cheated comes from the word Gypsies. Because that's what Gypsies do.

In Ireland, Romania, and other European countries the Gypsies travel in caravans and wear unusual clothing. They are called Tinkers or Traveling People. They are easy to see. In America they blend right in with the rest of us and we never know when they are around. But at least once a year the folks in Missouri get to see them come out of hiding and swarm together in one place.

Pictures of "Traveling People" in Europe

The story of Missouri's Gypsy swarm began in the summer of 1976 when the state was full of these travelers who were visiting the cities and towns with their schemes to get our money. One day a band of them were camping near the city of Rolla. Their Queen became very ill and died. After the ceremonies for her they took her into the City Cemetery in Rolla and bought a grave site. There she was buried with great dignity.

Eventually her husband, the King of the Gypsies also died and he was buried there beside his Queen. When the King was buried the other Gypsies propped him up in his casket with a big plate of food on his lap. He sat there while the others partied. He didn't eat anything.

As time went by other family members also died and were brought to the Rolla Cemetery to be with their Gypsy Royalty. Today you can visit their graves if you wish. They are surrounded by low white walls with white planters on the corners of each wall. The tombstones and planters are all decorated with dozens of bright red plastic roses.

Then each Memorial Day, the Gypsies from all over swarm to the graves and leave all sorts of strange decorations. They seem to leave an unusual number of carved wooden items – especially birds. For years, there was an old black purse on the Queen's tombstone and it was supposed to be cursed. It was there for a long time but it's gone now.

Traveling Home of an American Gypsy

There is another strange thing about those graves. For several years there were no names on the tombstones. Instead, in big letters carved into the stones, it said "BROADWAY." Why? I really don't know. Now the stones have names on them and two even have pictures of the deceased. Maybe someday I'll meet a Gypsy who can explain it all to me. For now, it's fun to have some mysteries around.

Daniel & Rebecca's Mystery Graves

Sometimes it's hard to find the graves of people from long ago. This is especially true of pioneer families who were on the frontier and had no way to purchase tombstones. Embalming hadn't been practiced yet and anything (or anyone) would quickly decompose once they were put in the ground. But famous people like Daniel Boone and his wife, Rebecca, should be different – right?

Well, that's true up to a point. You see, when old Dan'l died his family placed him in the family grave plot not far from his home. Rebecca was laid to rest there also and a large pink granite boulder marked the place. They even put a bronze plaque telling who was buried there.

Grave Marker for Dan'l and Rebecca Boone

Everything was fine until the state of Kentucky asked to have Daniel dug up and brought to the Bluegrass State for re-burial. "He's our greatest hero," they explained.

Daniel's family and other Missourians explained that he was a great hero for Missouri also. "Besides," they said, "Daniel hated Kentucky. He said the people there cheated him out of all of his land and possessions. Daniel said that he would never go back to Kentucky and we're not going to let him go now."

The two states went to court and somehow Kentucky won. So they sent a team of gravediggers to take the bodies of Mr. and Mrs. Boone back to Kentucky. When these people got to Marthasville, Missouri the Boone family showed them which two graves to dig up. The Kentuckians did their job and took the two bodies back to Kentucky. They buried the two skeletons in Kentucky soil and erected a huge monument over them.

A short time later the Boone family told everyone that they had pointed out the wrong two bodies and that Daniel and Rebecca were still buried in the family plot in Missouri after all. This started a huge argument that went on for years.

Finally forensic science got so good and DNA testing was so accurate that the authorities decided to dig up the bodies again and test them. This time they could find no DNA match to the Boone family descendants. So it appears that the old frontiersman got his wish after all. People in Kentucky won't agree to that. What do you think?

Recently a young idiot stole the brass plate from the granite boulder at the Boone grave. He had it melted down and sold for scrap metal. A new, more modern, plate was put in place by the Daughters of the American Revolution. That is the one pictured above.

Ha Ha Tonka

According to some, the words "Ha Ha Tonka" were taken from the Osage. It was supposed to mean "laughing waters."   It would be a good name for this place built above the Lake of the Ozarks. However, when it was built there was no Lake of the Ozarks. This castle sat high on a hill above the Osage River Valley and near a wonderful big spring.

Ha Ha Tonka Castle

I may be the only person in the world who thinks of this place in spooky terms. But, when I was a teenager, my friends and I would sit around inside this old castle at night and tell scary stories. One night we heard the loud shrill scream of a woman nearby. Everyone jumped up and looked wide-eyed at each other. Of course I wasn't scared but I'm sure everyone else was. OK, maybe I was at least as scared as anyone else. I think the scream was probably a cougar but I'll never know.

In the late 1800s Robert Snyder from Kansas City began purchasing land in this area and eventually owned 2500 acres! He was well-known in his day because, besides being very rich, he owned something called an automobile. His was one of the first in the state.

When Snyder had enough land he began his building project. He hired stone masons to come all the way from Scotland and build an actual castle on his Ozarks hilltop. Construction began in 1905.

Then, in 1906, Robert Snyder was killed in an automobile accident. His sons picked up the project and finished their father's dream castle. It was three stories tall, with a stone stable, nine greenhouses, and an eighty foot water tower. In those days the most impressive part of the castle was the Great Hall. (Just like in Scotland's castles.) Even today the Great Hall is still very impressive.

In 1942 disaster came again to the Snyder family. Sparks from the gigantic fireplace set the building afire. Now all that remains is the empty shell of the castle. But there is good news.

In 1978 Missouri bought the property with its castle, caves, springs, bluffs, and everything else. It is now probably the best state park that we all own. And today, if you get the chance, you can sit in the Great Hall and imagine how this author used to hear and tell ghost stories and how he almost jumped out of his pants one dark night when a cougar screamed.

There is another chapter to this story. Robert Snyder Jr., the son of the original builder, loved the stories about life in rural Missouri and Missouri folklore. He collected over a thousand books about this subject and kept them in the beautiful library in the castle. In his will he left the book collection to the Library of the University of Missouri – Kansas City.

Today many people use those books but some people feel that they are not there alone. They feel that they are being watched and claim to sometimes hear a rustling of pages nearby when they can see no one there. Is Mr. Snyder watching over his beloved collection?

Zombie Road

It's for sure – there are figures lurking on Zombie Road. By day this old road in Wildwood is a bicycle trail. By night, some will tell you that it's haunted by spirits. One story tells of American Indians who appear. Another tells of Rebels from the Civil War and one terrible story tells of packs of child ghosts. That's creepy enough to keep anyone away. Wrong!

In the old days this was an Indian trail leading to a good place to ford (cross) the river. Later it was known as the Lawler Ford Road, named for the Lawler family who lived nearby. For a hundred and fifty years or so people have been talking about the spooky place and going there to experience its frightening atmosphere.

Then, in 2007 a documentary hit the television channels called "Children of the Grave." It shows what the film-makers called "shadow people" which are only seen as dark silhouettes following people along the wooded hillsides. After that, even more people flocked to Zombie Road.

Now at night the place is full of mostly teenagers hoping to get spooked and see something they didn't expect and weren't prepared for. The St. Louis County Police have put up plenty of signs telling people to stay away but the teenagers still come, especially when it's near Halloween.

Almost all of the teenagers now can tell of very similar experiences. They enter the road at dark and the tree branches hang overhead completely obscuring any light from the moon or stars. The thick blackness of the place is truly creepy. Next they hear the rustling of leaves or what might even be footsteps nearby. At this point many of them turn and run. Those who don't always wish they had.

Because the footsteps are real! They are County Police officers arresting people for trespassing. The fine is anywhere from $300 to $1000 dollars plus court costs. But the teenagers keep coming.

****

Sam: Did you hear about the man who drowned last night in the city sewer?

Dan: That's awful! Was it an accident?

Sam: At first the police thought so – but now they're callling it a sewer-side.

Upper Blackwell Road

This little community is named for the Blackwell family who were early residents. It is said that Judge Blackwell had several people hanged from the old bridge on Upper Blackwell Road. Some say that the spirits of those poor souls are still at the site of the bridge. People also report that a cemetery there is haunted and that they have strange things happen in a restaurant there. The stories of the restaurant vary so wildly that it's hard to give much credit to any of them. Before the bridge was torn down there used to be stories of a mystery car that would appear and drive right at you.

There are two things that lots of the stories about this place have in common. One is that the temperature changes quickly and measurably at places along the road. The other is that several people have taken pictures in which "orbs" appear. These orbs of light look similar to those in the Lemp Mansion. A few people have also reported "dark spots" in places along the road.

Bone Hill

We have all heard those stories about how Native Americans only killed the few animals they needed for food and how they used every little bit of every animal in some way or another. It's a beautiful thought but it isn't true. That may be why large mammals like the mastodon and the giant bison are extinct. The Indians were opportunists and when they had a change to get extra food and supplies, they would act on it. Just like now, if someone has a chance to earn a big bonus at work, they will try to get it.

When the pioneers arrived in Missouri they found a place in Jackson County that they named Bone Hill. It was on this steep hill that the Indians would stampede the buffalo down the hill. Soon one buffalo would trip and fall causing others to fall over him and soon many dead and injured buffalo were laying at the bottom of the hill. By the time the pioneers got there, only the bleached out bones remained along with some arrowheads and hide-scraping tools.

A story is told that a pioneer family settled on that land and had their slaves clear the stones from the fields and stack them around the outside. This created a stone wall around their property. Then as the Missouri-Kansas border war got worse and the Civil War began this family sold their land for gold and moved away. We are told that they buried the gold near one part of the rock wall and it is said that they told friends and neighbors that they would return and see them in seven years.

No one remembers ever seeing that pioneer family again but in 1869, seven years after they left, a strange light began to appear out by the rock wall. People thought it was that family checking on the gold they had buried. Now it is said that the light returns and hovers around the rock wall every seven years.

Now, if this story is not true, what causes the light to appear? One theory concerns the layers of slate and limestone under the ground. This theory says that gasses build up and then ooze out every seven years. Honestly, does that sound like a good explanation to you?

If you would like to see the "seven year glimmer" for yourself you will need to be on Highway 24 near Levasy, Missouri on a dark night in 2016 or 2023. Maybe I'll see you there.

The Wives of Dan Dulany

Who was Dan Dulany? No one knows. But we do know a few things about him. We know that he was married at least three times and we know that he lived part of his life in Paris, Missouri. But no one there seemed to remember him when he was gone and he seems to have left no real records behind.

What he did leave behind was unlike anything in the world. He left three wives buried with one tombstone. His first wife was Jacinthia (Maupin) Dulany. She married Dan in 1841 and died in 1842. Next Dan married Ann Dulany. That was in 1851 and she died in 1853. Then he married Mary (Thompson) Dulany in 1845. She died later that same year. Is there a pattern?

Three-in-One Tombstone for the Dulany Wives

After that third wife died old Dan disappeared leaving nothing behind but that strange grave marker and lots of questions. Questions like:

* Where did Dan live before he came to Paris?

- Did he have any wives there?
- Where did he go when he left Paris?
- How many places did he travel to?
- Did he have any wives in those places? How many?
- Why can't anyone find information about this man? Did he change his name every time he moved?
- And of course the big question is just why did all these women die soon after marrying Dan?

The Hornersville Store

Hornersville is about as far south as you can go and still be in Missouri. It's on the southern edge of the Bootheel right at the Arkansas border. It's a tiny town but there was a time when The Hornersville Store was a very popular place to shop. People would travel from other states to the place. The attraction was the unusual store owners.

One owner was Named Captain Shadrack Shields. He was a former circus sideshow entertainer and measured seven feet, seven inches tall! For a time he was the tallest man in the world. The other owner was even more famous.

The second owner's name was William "Major" Ray. William and his wife were famous as the world's smallest couple. Major was only three feet, seven inches tall! He worked for the Brown Shoe Company in St. Louis and was known across America as Buster Brown, the little boy who lived in a shoe. There were comic books, movies and all sorts of things about Buster Brown.

So when people shopped at the Hornersville Store they were greeted by the tallest man in the world and a famous man who happened to be one of the shortest people in the world. What a pair! If you could, wouldn't you go in there? I sure would! But of course these people lived about a hundred years ago so I suppose we've missed our chance.

Wright County Courthouses

In 1849 the Courthouse was burned. Well bad things sometimes happen. However, it burned again in 1862. Then Civil War soldiers burned the new Courthouse in 1863. They moved into a temporary Courthouse but it burned in 1864. Then in 1888 a terrible tornado came through Hartville and, you guessed it, there went the Courthouse. At least it wasn't another fire. Would you believe that in 1896 they had another fire at the Courthouse. Well, it happened. But in 1897 it happened again!

The Wright County Courthouse was destroyed seven times! Some courthouses in other Missouri counties burned several times but not that many times. There were many reasons why courthouses would burn.

As with the Wright County buildings, some military soldiers would set fire to the courthouse as punishment to those in a place where they thought the enemy lived. It was a way to punish the local people. It was just plain mean.

And, of course, there are natural and accidental fires. In America's early days it also used to be fairly common for lawyers and people being sued to set fires and destroy records which could be harmful to them in a trial. Without the records, you couldn't be convicted.

This writer was a little surprised in preparing this book that no Missouri courthouses are supposed to be haunted. After all, that is where they used to hang people in the old days. Sometimes they would build a scaffold on the lawn so everyone could watch. Other courthouses had trap doors in the floors so they could put a noose on the person's neck and drop them through. Most of those trap doors have now been covered over or hidden because we don't like to think about unpleasant things any more. But with all those executions of murderers and other mean people, wouldn't you think some stories would have popped up about wild spirits "hanging around?"

Strange Animals

Hoop Snakes

When I was still a boy in the Ozarks my father warned me to beware of hoop snakes. They were said to have a painful bite and, if aggravated, they were hard to avoid. I was told that, no matter how fast you might run, you could not get away from them. The only thing you can do is to hide behind a tree.

What makes the snake so hard to escape from is his ability to hold his tail in his mouth and roll like a hula hoop faster than anyone can run. I've been watching for many years and have never yet seen one. In fact, no one I know has ever seen one. Do they exist?

Well the naturalist, Raymond Ditmars, has put $10,000.00 in the bank for anyone who can show him a specimen of the snake. The money is still there but no one has been able to produce a hoop snake. Let's train a black snake to do the trick and get rich!

Sea Serpent

Back in August of 1877 a St. Louis newspaper said that several noted scientists were interested in reports of a "sea Serpent" which had been sighted in the Mississippi River. It was described as about 30 feet long with dark scales, a head like a dog and a mouth like a pelican.

Just picture that in your head or, better yet, try to draw something like that. A snake's body, a dog's head, and a pelican's beak! I have never seen such a thing and I certainly hope I never do!

Snot Otters

Can you imagine going to a nice Ozark stream and finding a creature as big as an otter but this one is all covered with a clear slime? He looks like a two-foot-long booger with legs and a face!

Snot Otters will never win a beauty contest but I love them just the same. These two-foot-long slimy salamanders live in our cleanest Ozark streams. Pioneers who encountered them often didn't know just what they were so they gave them some pretty colorful names. My favorite name is "snot otters."

Other people called them things like "devil dog", "mud-devil", "grampus", or "mud dog." In truth, almost everybody now calls them "hellbenders."

A Snot Otter

In spite of their scary-sounding names, they are very gentle creatures and never hurt anybody. They are in danger of becoming extinct because those beautiful Ozark streams that they love just happen to be the kinds of places that we love. So, as we build vacation homes and resorts, we stir up the mud and the spaces between the rocks in the riverbed fill in with sand and dirt. Those spaces are the homes of the hellbenders so they are quickly loosing their habitat.

Probably the worst enemies of these critters are the ATVs and monster trucks that people love to drive through the rivers and streams. These "mud rallies" make the water so dirty that fish and water creatures can't get the oxygen they need. Hellbenders used to be very common in many streams. There are only about 750 of them left in the Ozarks now.

So the next time someone tells you that there is no such thing as a snot otter, you speak right up and set them straight. Tell that person that you like snot otters and want to protect the environment for them. They might still think you're crazy but – crazy and nice.

Buzzards

Oh, sure! You already know all about buzzards! Maybe not. Did you know that there are no buzzards in this state at all. What people around here call buzzards are really vultures. Almost all of the vultures we have are Turkey Vultures but along the Arkansas border there are a few black vultures as well. And these are some of the grossest and most fascinating creatures you can imagine.

Vultures have very special digestive systems. They mix the very rotten meat they eat with gastric juices so strong that they even kill the germs and bacteria in the rotten food. They eat things that no other birds or mammals can.

When they find a big enough carcasses they gorge themselves and get so full and so heavy that they can't fly anymore. They have to just sit there and let everything digest before they can leave. In the meantime they are very vulnerable to dogs, coyotes, and other predators. If a predator approaches, the vulture can vomit like a fire hose and direct the rotten acidic mess into the face of the predator. This also makes the vulture lighter so it can now take off and fly to safety.

Another unique behavior keeps them cool. Vultures cannot sweat to cool off so they squirt a combination of defecation and urine onto their legs and feet. The acid in the urine kills any germs that they may have picked up from the dead animals they eat. As the mess evaporates from the legs and feet, it takes heat away and cools the birds. This is why their yellow legs and feet always look gray.

I really thought that we had a group of vultures using our barn for a roost. Actually, they are only sitting up on top early in the morning to sun themselves. They also gather on top of the old barn just before they fly off to their well-hidden roosting tree. I wondered why I couldn't find their nests in the barn. Well, it's because they don't build nests. They just lay their eggs next to a stump or a rock.

White Squirrels

OK. I admit it. There's nothing scary or mysterious about this story. It's just something a little bit strange in Missouri. If you are ever near Marionville, you really should take a minute and stop in the town. You will notice all sorts of nice trees especially selected and grown to make squirrels happy. And the squirrels in Marionville are special.

They are not albinos but they are pure white and fluffy and friendly. There are a couple of other towns in other states with white squirrels but they aren't as big and there aren't as many. Marionville truly has something special here.

White Squirrels

The Ozark Howler

The Ozark Howler may be a very real critter but not necessarily one that we don't already know. It has been described as a very large member of the cat family. Those who claim to have seen it say that it is larger than any feral cat, bobcat, or even a cougar. In fact, it is supposed to be bigger than any dog.

Witnesses say that it is black and makes loud howling noises. Some claim that it has large horns on its head. You understand that a mountain lion (cougar) seen at night will appear to have dark fur. In this case, however, the fur is said to be long and shaggy – more like a bear than a mountain lion. Its body is also different from the mountain lion because, instead of long, thin, and graceful, the Ozark Howler's body is supposed to be thick, stocky, and powerful.

"Devil Cat" is the name given to it in parts of the Ozarks. This is because of the two horns protruding from its head. The sudden, bone-chilling, go-home-and-change-your-underwear howl is another reason for the devilish name. So far, no one has produced an Ozark Howler either dead or alive but that is what it will take to answer this mystery. Imagining myself in a dark Ozark forest at night, I can tell you that I wouldn't want to see one or even hear one. I sure wouldn't stay around hoping to get one to bring home!

Could this prehistoric mammal be the Ozark Howler?

When Cows Fly

Elm Farm Ollie was a cow who made history back in 1930. She became the first cow to fly in an airplane. Her plane took off from Bismarck, Missouri and flew to St. Louis. On that day Elsworth Bunce became the first man to milk a cow in the air. The milk was put into paper containers with small parachutes and then dropped to people in the city below. It was an advertising stunt for the dairy that sponsored the event.

Houn' Dawgs

When this writer was a boy I used to hear a funny song about a farm boy whose dog was being mistreated by some town boys. Then one day those town boys bullied the farm boy and the dog came to his rescue. Well, I had no idea about what a famous dog that was.

You see, down in Taney County they sang that song about the good old hound dog. Then in 1891 the Second Missouri Division of the U.S. Army was formed and as they traveled around the country they took that song of the loyal and protective hound. The song continued with the group and by 1918 the other soldiers in World War I called this Missouri division The Houn' Dawgs.

Many Missouri soldiers have served in the Houn' Dawg units through several wars and they have always been as tough and as dedicated as that good old farm dog from Taney County. At this writing the 203rd Missouri National Guard proudly carries that name into battle in Afghanistan.

Ev'ry time I come to town
The boys keep kickin' my dawg aroun';
Makes no diff'rence if he is a houn',
They gotta quit kickin' my dawg aroun'.

Me an' Lem Briggs an' old Bill Brown
Took a load of corn to town;
My old Jim dawg, onery old cuss,
He just naturally follered us.

As we driv past Johnson's store
A passel of yaps come out the door;
Jim he scooted behind a box
With all them fellers a-throwin' rocks.

They tied a can to old Jim's tail
An' run him past the county jail;
That just naturally made us sore,
Lem, he cussed an' Bill he swore.

Me an' Lem Briggs an' old Bill Brown
Lost no time a-gittin' down;
We wiped them fellers on the ground
For kickin' my old Jim dawg around.

Jim seen his duty there an' then,
He lit into them gentlemen;
He shore mussed up the court-house square
With rags an' meat an' hide an' hair.

Today the sports teams in Aurora, Missouri are called the Houn' Dawgs in honor of the famous Ozarks canine.

Lions & Turkeys & Bears – Oh My!

Before I go much further with my stories I want to tell you something about the way Missouri used to be. This writer grew up on a farm in the Ozarks about twelve miles from the nearest town. But, even way out there in the boonies, I never saw a wild deer or a wild turkey. Of course we had no bears, mountain lions or other large mammals.

When I was in college I had a professor who told us that the deer population was coming back and that they would attract predators like mountain lions and maybe even wolves. He predicted that these predators would find their way down the Missouri River Valley and then along other smaller rivers into the Ozarks. He also predicted the large-scale repopulation of turkeys.

He was right about every single one of those things. The deer and turkey are so thick now that they have become a nuisance in many places. Wildlife cameras have taken clear pictures of black bears and mountain lions. Of course many individuals have seen them also.

My only experience with a bear happened when I was camping on my cousin's farm in Laclede County. Although I was afraid to come out of my tent to see him, a bear rummaged through my camp one night. I had only a pocket knife to protect myself so I stayed still in the tent but, when he was gone, his paw prints were very clear. My point is that creatures which did not exist in the Ozarks only a few years ago now inhabit the hills in huge numbers. What else might turn up in places like the Mark Twain National Forests?

Panthers

Back in July of 1875 the Carthage Banner newspaper was reporting a problem with "panthers" killing livestock. Hunting parties were being formed and it was hoped that they could kill at least a dozen of the big cats. As you know, what some people call panthers, other people call cougars, or mountain lions. The Indians called them Pumas.

By any name they are predators and meat eaters. They would usually kill mostly deer but when the deer were being killed off by settlers the cats would find what ever they could. Domestic livestock didn't really know how to fight back so they were easy prey for the panthers.

Eventually the big cats were eliminated from Missouri's farm country but now the deer are back so we are seeing more and more mountain lions. If you ever see one, back away and leave. Also be sure to tell the local sheriff.

Booger Dogs

According to the people who know about booger dogs, they are supposed to be big and black and a lot like a dog but they are different in some ways. The booger dog is eight feet long and has a big lump of a thing where its head should be. The eyes, nose, mouth, and ears are on this big lump. These creatures are also known as hellhounds, devil dogs, and demon dogs. But in Missouri, they are always booger dogs.

A Springfield area man, S M Belekurov, seems to have done the most research about booger dogs and he writes of sightings in his area. In his appearances on local radio programs he tells of twelve sightings in the areas of Nixa, Republic, Ozark, Bois D'Arc, Marshfield, Camdenton, Rogersville, Branson and Mincy. The most famous sighting is one people call "Paul, the Nixa Hellhound" but Belekurov thinks Paul is probably an April Fool's hoax. However, he also feels that four of the sightings are different from the others and they match the descriptions of booger dogs that we've heard over many generations.

Stories over the years have several things in common. One is that these dogs always stay near roads. They also are said to be as "big as a buck" and very stocky. Every account tells of these animals having eyes much larger than normal.

An interesting story is told in Southwest Missouri. There was said to be an old farmer named Wolfe. He was sort of the neighborhood grouch and would never help others. He was a stingy, selfish, miserly, old hermit. He never went to church and the neighbors called him a blasphemer. When someone would say his last name, they would quickly spit as if his name left a bad taste in their mouths.

When the day came that it looked as if the old man was about to die, a large group of neighbors went to his home hoping to help him and maybe save his bitter soul. As they talked about religion lightning struck the house and it was quickly enveloped in flames. The neighbors all ran out but four strong men stayed to carry Wolfe outside. These four strong men couldn't lift the little old man from his bed. Then they tried to pick up the entire bed but it wouldn't budge.

Finally they were forced to run outside but, just as they did, a huge black dog ran through the door past them and disappeared into the woods. No one could remember seeing a gigantic dog in the house. Then, when the ashes cooled, folks went into the house to recover the old man's body and bury it. But, you guessed it, there was no body in the ashes.

Now these are stories and reported sightings but a detective would say, "What are the clues? What do these things have in common?" Over hundreds of years hellhounds or booger dog sightings seem to have some common elements. For one, they all seem to happen along roads and highways. This is true of Highway 65 in Missouri but along other roads in Europe.

They also seem to happen between 36° and 38° degrees of north latitude. These stories often contain mention of fire, electricity, or lightning. Mr. Belekurov mentioned above has noted that several of the most modern happenings were just after storms with thunder and lightning.

Gigantic Fish

As a boy this writer spent a lot of time at Bennett Spring. There, 72 million gallons of cold clean clear water gushed out of a deep blue hole every day. It was and is a wonderful and fascinating place. There were many stories told of attempts to enter the depths of the spring and find out what was down there and where the water was coming from.

My favorite story was of a time when scuba divers put on heavy weights and swam downward fighting the upward current of the water. They reached a point where flint and other rocks were swirling around violently and striking the divers. They could go no further.

However, at that point the story says, they saw huge rainbow trout. There, with plenty of food and total safety from the hooks of fishermen, they were free to grow to an enormous size. At least that's the story that was told.

It is certainly true however that the depths of some Missouri waters do produce fish as big as people. I've actually seen some of those and many photographs exist to show others.

Greg Bernal and Jonet Momphard were fishing one day when they pulled in a monster blue catfish that weight 130 pounds! That is certainly larger than a lot of people. It was 45 inches around. How big around is your waist?

Even bigger are the fish people call the spoonbill or paddlefish. One of those was caught in the James River part of Table Rock Lake and it weighed 139 pounds and 4 ounces!

Spoonbills are also called Paddlefish

Besides looking just plain weird, these fish have no bones and no scales. They almost have no eyes. The eyes they do have are really tiny. But the big spoon things on the front of them are huge. Paddlefish are fresh water relatives of sharks but they don't hunt or kill their food and they don't even eat other fish. They eat plankton. Like their shark cousins, they detect food in the water by feeling electric impulses from them.

If you look at the picture above but cover up the "paddle" on his nose, he even looks like a shark.

If you remember this next part, you will know something that most people don't know about paddlefish. They don't use those big paddles to stir up mud and look for food. The paddles are full of electrical receptors just like sharks have on their noses. The paddles get "tingly" when food is around.

Paddlefish are in trouble right now because they need clear streams to lay their eggs and because those eggs can be made into caviar. Caviar is so good and worth so much money that people take the eggs rather than let them hatch. This is one reason that people are no longer supposed to try to catch the monsters.

Paddlefish Filtering Food from the Water

It's interesting to know that, since the fish are filter feeders, they aren't interested in any kind of bait you could put on a hook. So, when people did catch the big fish, they would usually do it with arrows or spears.

A truly monsterous fish is the alligator gar. This thing has two rows of large teeth in his upper jaw which make him look something like an alligator. His scales are huge diamond-shaped things and very tough. The Indians used to use his scales for arrowheads.

Adult alligator gar can be ten feet long and can weigh over 200 pounds. One bowfisherman brought in a 365 pound gator gar! They are carnivors and they lurk in shallow water until their meal comes by. Sometimes these monsters are said to have attacked people but that has never been verified. Just take a look at the picture below of one that was cought back in 1910. Would you want to be in the river with that?

Alligator Gar

****

While we're talking about Missouri animals, let me mention Kennett, Missouri. Did you know that in April of 2012 Kennett was starting an Alligator Roundup all over town? Some traveling salesman sold a bunch of baby alligators as pets and the folks in Kennett started raising them until they got too big to be cute (or safe) so they let them loose. Growing hungry alligators are not a good thing to have around your nice neighborhood!

Jim the Wonder Dog

They say that the average dog can understand about 100 words. We've all seen things that certain dogs can do that are impressive, but the most impressive doge ever was known as Jim the Wonder Dog.

Jim lived in Marshall, Missouri back in 1925. He was more than just a really smart animal. We've all seen those but Jim was something special. Listen to some of the feats that Jim could routinely perform.

When hunting he knew which fields had birds in them and which ones did not. Samuel Van Arsdale, Jim's owner, just let Jim choose the fields for hunting and he said he was never disappointed.

You probably know that dogs are color blind. They can only see black and white and shades of gray. But Jim was different. You could put objects in any order and change the order but Jim could always pick out whatever color you asked him to find.

Jim could also find people's cars for them. All you had to do was to tell him the license plate number and he'd go right to it. You could tell him the make of the car and it's color and he'd find it for you. You could even point out the owner of the car and he would find the correct car. He may have been doing that one by scent.

If you would ask him to find a particular kind of tree or shrub, he would find one for you. He could even locate a business for you if you would tell him the name.

Since dogs can't speak, answers would often have to be written on papers for him. He could always choose the paper with the correct answer. In case you think his owner was tipping him off, the answers were sometimes written in languages Mr. Van Arsdale didn't understand. Jim correctly responded to answers written in English, Italian, French, German, Greek, and Spanish.

In 1936 they decided to see if Jim could pick the winner in the presidential election. Of course he did. They also asked him to indicate who would win the World Series and he did that correctly too.

He was so good at predicting, the people decided to see if he could predict the winner for the Kentucky Derby. He did. He also did the next year and the next. They asked him to choose the winner for seven years and he was correct all seven times. As if there were no limits to his abilities, he could routinely indicate correctly the sex of a baby before it was born.

Scientists and veterinarians at the University of Missouri in Columbia examined Jim. Except for the fact that he responded to their commands given in five different languages, he seemed normal in every way. I wouldn't say "normal" would you?

If you go to Marshall, Missouri some day, you will want to go to Jim the Wonder Dog Park and see the statue of this amazing animal.

Jim the Wonder Dog Statue

Strange Practices

Divining

How is it that some of the smartest people I know have come to believe in the practice of finding water, minerals, graves, and other things by a strange, seemingly magical process called "divining?" As I mentioned, they came to the belief — they didn't start out believing. Many people who were skeptical have now changed their minds.

Called divining, dowsing, and water witching, the process always has certain things that are necessary. The "dowser" uses a forked stick, a bowed stick, or two rods held parallel to each other. No one can tell you why it happens but they all agree on how it happens. The universal signal seems to be the rods pulling downward toward the person's feet when they are over the water or other desired object.

The divining rods can be made of several kinds of wood or certain metals. Each dowser has his or her own favorite. There seems to be no difference in abilities when it comes to men or women. Either can be very successful with divining and even children can often do this if they are patient. Everyone develops his or her own style.

We usually hear of divining for water or minerals but there are other options. I manage two historic cemeteries and many of the oldest graves are not marked with stones. Some of the oldest stones are too worn to be read. Therefore, I sometimes encounter people who need help in locating old graves. A few specially-trained dogs can do this but a much more common practice is to have diviners walk the area.

In Laclede County Lillian Humphreys has repeatedly demonstrated not only her ability to find underground water but also her ability to tell exactly how far down the well must be dug in order to reach the water.

One common phenomenon is that of the person who cannot get results when trying to dowse. This person then tries again with a successful dowser touching the first person's back or shoulder. All of a sudden, the first person can experience the same success as the real dowser.

Now water can be located with ground penetrating radar and with instruments suspended from airplanes or helicopters. How expensive would that be? Professional well drillers say that it is fairly common for people to choose the location of a new well and have water witching as a part of the location process. There may be another large percentage of people who consult the dowser before a driller is ever called.

I often read through articles from the past. They explain old-fashioned practices which were common then but now seem strange or even silly. I would love to be able to read this a hundred years from now and see if divining is still practiced or if it is considered the stuff of witch doctors. My guess is that it will still be used for one reason: it seems to work.

Turkey Boots and Pigs' Eyes

Speaking of things going out of practice: In the past there were no trucks to haul animals to market so people called "drovers" would group them together and drive them down the country roads, across grasslands and even through the woods. You have seen people do this in movies with cattle but cattle are easy. They like to stay together in herds. Pigs and turkeys are very independent and like to run or fly away.

Getting them across a river or stream was especially hard. Can you imagine trying to get a turkey to swim? Of course you would have to have a raft waiting and you would still plan on losing many of your animals.

You probably realize that a hundred or more years ago most turkeys and pigs didn't wear hiking boots or even sneakers. But their feet were not and are not made for traveling on gravel roads. How on earth could you solve these problems and get the animals to market?

Well, our ancestors were clever and inventive people so here are a couple of tricks they invented. One was turkey boots. They would force the turkeys to walk through warm (not hot) tar. This is the black sticky stuff they use to pave roads and highways. As the turkeys walked through the tar would stick to their feet. From the tar pit there was only one way to leave and that was through a sand box. The sand would stick to the tar and each turkey would then be surprised to see that he or she was wearing a new little pair of "boots." It sounds silly but it protected their feet on the gravel roads.

Now the pigs had a different problem. They were just so independent that they looked for every chance to run away into the woods. That's why we have feral pigs in the Ozarks today. So, if you were a drover back then, how would you make the pigs stay together?

The solution they came up with was a very strange one indeed! They took a needle and thread and, with just one stitch, they sewed the eyelids closed on those pigs. Now, since the pigs couldn't see, they couldn't run away. This made them much easier to drive. It didn't hurt the pigs more than just a little sting and, as soon as they got to the stockyards, they would snip the thread and the pigs could see again. Sewing pigs' eyelids is one job that I hope I never have to do!

Bringing Turkeys to Market

More Farm Animals

Farmers and ranchers are very independent people. Not all of them think about things in the same way their neighbors do. Some raise huge herds of animals that might surprise us. In 1917 the *Chillicothe Constitution* reported that C. C. Hoyt had bought and sold 12,000 rabbits within the past week.

In 1910 the Cassville Republican reported that a farmer near Madry in Barry County was hard at work setting up his new farm. His plan was to raise and sell thousands of skunks.

This writer wondered why anyone would operate a skunk farm. It turns out that many people used to think skunks were good pets and some still do. There is still at least one very modern skunk farm raising de-scented pets for sale.

Ozark Child Rearin'

Here's a challenge for you. Go to any really old church and glance at their records from the 1800s. You will see an amazing number of infant deaths. Little kids have always had a hard time getting through infancy but it is not always just because of natural reasons. Our strange beliefs also play a part.

In the Ozarks it was believed that children, if they were to survive, must develop a case of hives while they were still infants. For the first few days after childbirth, mothers were still weak so infant care was done by the oldest daughter, the granny, or whoever was available to help. In order to bring on the hives, people would give the babies special teas made of sheep manure or mouse parts. These remedies were often fatal.

One lady sighed and sadly said, "I probably killed several of my little brothers and sisters." She was the oldest daughter and was responsible for giving teas to the infants.

One woman, describing various worm teas made of catnip, onions, and Jerusalem oak seeds, said, "It would pretty near kill you, let alone the worms. It would really get rid of them."

Stomach bands were considered essential for newborns. These cotton bands were worn for protection until the umbilical cord dropped off. Babies were not allowed to cry loudly or for very long because this might cause the navel to stick out. I guess they preferred "insies."

We've all seen pictures from the days when all of the children wore dresses – yes, even the boys! That made it easier to change the babies' diapers. It also allowed room for a diaper pad, which was an old blanket to soak up overflows. To avoid tripping, dresses got shorter as the little ones began to walk.

Many older people still remember shirts, dresses and clothing made from carefully selected feed and flour bags. These would often be printed with bright flowers, plaids, or paisley designs. We loved it when we got to choose our own sacks. Ask your grandmother if she remembers this.

One day, when discussing bent-over "thong trees," an old timer told me that it was common in the early days to bend over a sapling and tie it down so the boys could bounce on it like a toy horse. They had to make their own playground equipment back then.

Living in a rural home meant that a mother would sometimes have to come up with ways to occupy little children for a few minutes while she tended to other things. One way was to make a little pacifier called a sugar tit. Another way was to give the child a feather with molasses on it. It would stick to one hand and then the other for long periods of time.

This writer remembers well my grandmother's way of keeping me and my cousins busy. First was to let us go outside and be kids. If we ever got a little too wild . . . When we got a little too wild, she would call us in and sit us around the big dinner table. Then out would come the jars of buttons.

We never knew why Grandma needed all those buttons strung on long strings and arranged by size or color. We never thought to ask. We just respected her so much that when she needed help with her button stringing chores, we did everything we could to help.

Of course she was just getting us to settle down for a while. After a few minutes of stringing, a reminder to behave, and maybe a little snack, we were back outside and playing. Child rearin' Ozark-style was sometimes strange and even deadly but sometimes it was a wonderful thing!

Ozark Cousins

Snake Bite

It was a little bit unusual when some guys down in Cassville caught a rattle snake but what they did with it was truly strange. The *Carthage Banner* newspaper reported in 1874 that two men had captured a rattlesnake that was six feet, seven inches long. It had twenty-seven rattles!

Then, since they knew that it was against the law to sell whiskey in that area, except for medicine, they offered a plan. For fifteen cents they would let the snake bite you and then they would let you have one drink of "medicine." The newspaper doesn't say how many people wanted to pay to get poisoned by the snake. Do you think many people did?

Still More Strange Stuff

Meet Me in St. Louie, Louie. Meet Me at the Fair.

Much of this information was supplied via the internet by Joe Sonderman.

I'll bet that more than a thousand books have been written about the 1904 St. Louis World's Fair! It was a wondrous and wonderful thing. It was held at the end of the Old West era and the beginning of the electronic age. Many people came to St. Louis to see electric lights for the first time. Most of them saw flying machines for the first time. Visitors from the East and from Europe came to see cowboys and Indians. And all of the visitors were amazed by sights brought in from all over the world.

Some countries brought entire villages of their native people and set them up to live at the fair as exhibits. Most interesting among these turned out to be the tribe from the Philippines who have people still talking about them over a hundred years later.

I have listed below a sort of timeline concerning the World's Fair. It shows only the tiniest fraction of the things that happened but it does include some of the strangest things and that is what we want for this book.

Two of the biggest issues prior to opening the Fair were cleaning up the city so it would look good for visitors and finding enough good drinking water for everyone. It took several years of hard work but, just in the nick of time, water was found and the city looked good to everyone arriving at Union Station.

Another major problem before the opening of the Fair was that some of the other nations, especially Russia, weren't being very cooperative. As a result the Fair, planned for 1903, didn't actually happen until 1904.

August 20, 1902 – The first birth and the first death occurred on the World's Fair Grounds on this day. Louisiana Purchase O'Leary was the strange name of a girl born to Mr. and Mrs. Larry O'Leary. The baby lived for nearly a hundred years. Her father was a construction worker at the Fair.

A few hours later a man rigging equipment, Alfred Willis, died when a sledgehammer fell 75 feet and struck him on the head. It sounds awful but at least he never knew what happened and felt no pain. A sledgehammer? 75 feet?

September 11, 1903 – The St. Louis *Globe-Democrat* was commenting on a plan to cool the World's Fair when it said, it was probably a good idea but would not be surprised to find out that artificially cooled buildings were unhealthy, "since we know by experience that everything nice is unhealthy." They were already learning that every time someone tries to do something to make life better, someone else comes along and says that it's not good for us. Thankfully the folks at the fair went ahead and "air-cooled" the buildings. Before the invention of air-conditioning, it was the best they could do.

April 30, 1904 – The Louisiana Purchase Exposition opened in St. Louis one year behind schedule. (Of course most of us call it the St. Louis World's Fair.) A crowd of 200,000 was on hand for the opening ceremonies. John Phillip Sousa brought the Marine Corps Band, Presidents Teddy Roosevelt and William Taft were there along with massed bands, and 10,000 flags were flying!

On March 25, 1904 – Before the fair opened, the most popular and famous people at the World's Fair arrived by train. They were the dog-eating, head-hunting, "wild people" from the Philippines. Folks didn't know what to think about them. Some people refused to visit the area at all. Many men wouldn't let their wives and daughters see the scantily-clad people.

March 29, 1904 – The Igorot (Philippine) people at the World's Fair proved themselves not to be shy. They didn't like the food being provided for them so on this day they asked their contact man for a favor. The contact man then requested that the master of the dog pound supply eight dogs per day to the Igorots. May people around St. Louis were very upset to hear that the tribe would be killing dogs and eating them.

Actually, the way it worked out, so many people were talking about the Igorot that it made even more people want to come by and check them out.

It should also be mentioned that dogs have been considered good food in much of the world all through history. When the Spanish first came to the New World they found the Native Americans were eating dogs so the Spanish gave it a try. They liked one kind of dog meat so much that that particular breed is now extinct. The Spaniards ate them all up. Let's also remember that, in his first book, President Obama told about how he ate dog meat when he was a boy in Indonesia.

April 4, 1904 – The Women's Humane Society heard the results of an investigation which showed that the Igorot people who were eating dogs at the World's Fair killed the dogs by beating them to death. The women suggested that the Igorats be supplied with canned dog meat which was readily available. Why would canned dog meat be "readily available" in Missouri at that time – or any time? Who would use canned dog meat? I've never bought any – have you?

April 10, 1904 – Inflation was becoming a problem at the World's Fair. Governor Hunt of the Philippine Village complained that he was paying $2.00 for dogs that normally wouldn't bring ten cents. So, when people would buy and sell dogs, it would be for ten cents or less? Was there a big business going on buying and selling cheap dogs? This all makes me wonder.

April 14, 1904 – Seven Teheulche Indians arrived at the World's Fair from Patagonia. They demanded, and got, a diet of horse meat. As if things weren't bad enough for animal lovers, now they want horses roasting on the fire. What's next.

(I'll bet none of them ask for snot otters.) Of course horse meat is still eaten in many parts of the world including places as close as Canada. And here in the U.S. we know that our explorers and mountain men often were forced to eat their horses to stay alive. That's why many of them refused to give their horses names. It's hard to eat something with a name.

April 19, 1904 – A baby girl was born in the Philippine Village at the World's Fair. A girl as your first baby was considered bad luck so the infant was ignored by the parents and she died a few days later. This shocked many Americans but it was a common practice in many parts of the world. Aren't you glad you live in America?

May 23, 1904 – Missouri's Governor and the World Fair's President made a gift of some ice cream to the Bontoc people. (Bontocs were a group of Igorots from the Chico River area of the Philippines.) The Bontocs refused to try the strange food because it was cold. So the officials held the Bontocs down and forced the ice cream down their throats. How rude! This was not politically correct but back then people didn't worry so much about those things. The Bontocs still didn't like the ice cream and we can only imagine what terrible things they thought about the Governor and his friend.

A Bontoc Igorot Man

May 24, 1904 – The Ferris Wheel at the World's Fair was tested on this day. It stood 25 stories tall and could carry 2000 people. It had 36 cars and each of them was as large as a modern city bus. The axle was the largest piece of forged steel in the world.

The Giant Ferris Wheel

June 5, 1904 – 8000 people paid to see the bull fight at the arena. (part of the World's Fair) Some people complained that bullfighting was cruel to the bulls so the St. Louis County Sheriff stopped the show. This really upset the 8000 people who had paid their money and given up their day at the Fair to see the Spectacle of the Bulls. The angry crowd burned the building to the ground.

The man who promoted the event quickly put on a disguise and left with the all the customer's money. That left the matador and his assistant un-paid and arguing over money. On the 8th the assistant killed the Matador. Fun at the Fair!

By the way, don't you think it's funny to invite people from all over the world to come to America and show us what they do in their countries and then expect them to act like Americans? This writer hates bullfighting but I also know that when I went to some countries, fighting the bulls and showing your bravery and skill was a part of their lives.

June 6, 1904 – The Apache Chief, Geronimo, arrived in St. Louis to sign autographs and pose for pictures at the World's Fair. This was extremely important because people had come from all over America to see the various Indian nations and their leaders. Geronimo had only surrendered a few years earlier and people were very curious about him.

Many people had come from other countries and they wanted to see cowboys and Indians when they got to America. They especially wanted to see the most famous ones. Geronimo had been staying away until the Fair agreed to pay him more money and finally, he won and got what he wanted.

Sometimes we hear stories about how much everyone loved the rides and especially the Ferris wheel. Well, not everyone did. Geronimo, one of the bravest of people, was one person who didn't like riding on the Ferris Wheel.

June 18, 1904 – Members of the cast of a Wild West Show got involved in an actual shootout at the World's Fair. Amazingly, they were doing the show with real bullets and one cowboy was wounded and one bystander was killed. While this sounds just awful, remember that people had come to see cowboys and Indians and they were thrilled to write home and say there had been a real wild west shootout in the Outlaw State.

June 21, 1904 – It was announced that one car on the World's Fair Ferris Wheel would be set aside just for weddings. It could hold 60 people and a piano. This seems tame by our standards. Now we see on the television where people are getting married while they sky dive or ride roller coasters. But this was the thing back then. Can you imagine it being kind of nice? It was a very popular thing to do.

June 24, 1904 – The War Department ordered the primitive people at the World's Fair to wear more clothing. (Yes, the War Department. I know it doesn't make sense but it's true.) Why did the Generals and Admirals care how people from other countries are dressed? And, again, why did they invite people here to show us what they were like and then expect them to dress and act like Americans?

June 30, 1904 – A group of African pygmies arrived at the World's Fair. Ota Benga became the best known of the group and, he loved being in America. Some officials from New York told him that they would love to have him stay in their city. They told him that, if he would just live there, they would give him a place to stay in a big park and he could always have plenty of food and water. After the fair, he went to New York and they put him on display in the monkey house at the Bronx zoo. He shot himself in 1916.

July 1, 1904 – The Olympic Games began in St. Louis. When we think of the Olympic Games, it's hard to imagine that they were just a small part of the gigantic World's Fair. Of course it was different back then but it's an amazing thing just the same.

August 14, 1904 – Humane Society officials tried to arrest cowboys and Indians at the World's Fair for roping and tying cattle. The cowboys and Indians attacked the officers and the fans joined in when the show was temporarily canceled. Remember, these weren't police officers trying to arrest the cowboys and Indians – they were Humane Society people. It must have been a shock when the cowboys and Indians and thousands of fans all came after them! They probably should have thought about that first.

August 15, 1904 – Things settled down at the cowboy and Indians show and they were back to roping cattle. 76-year-old Geronimo was roping calves on this day. He did very well and got a good round of applause from the audience.

August 17, 1904 – George Eyser had a good day competing in the Gymnastics events at the Olympic Games in St. Louis. He won gold in the parallel bars, and rope climb, and tied for gold in the vault. He won silver on the pommel horse and the all-around. He took the bronze medal on the horizontal bars. Pretty good for a guy with one wooden leg!

If you ever start to feel sorry for yourself, think of George Eyser. Trying to complete while being off-balance because of having only one leg, he still managed to capture 3 gold medals, 2 silver medals, and one bronze. What a guy!

August 28, 1904 – Blinded by dust, famous racecar driver, Barney Oldfield lost control of his "Green Dragon" and slammed into a fence at the Fairground Race Track in St. Louis. The car cut one spectator in half and killed another. Oldfield felt so terrible that he never raced again. Crashes are a part of racing but in those days cars were still something fairly new. The cars weren't as safe as they are now and neither were the grandstands.

August 29, 1904 – Track and Field events began at the St. Louis Olympic Games. A new event, the decathlon, was won by an Irishman, Tom Kiely. George Poage became the first black man ever to compete in the Olympics and he liked St. Louis so much that he decided to stay to coach and teach at Sumner High School.

September 9, 1904 – The Olympics were now over but some results were still in question. The Milwaukee team was found to be professionals so they had to give up their gold medal for tug-of-war. But, wait a minute, they were tug-of-war professionals? How could you be a tug-of-war professional? Did people really pay to see other people pull on a rope? Was there a National Tug Of War League? This all makes me think of that goofy movie about professional dodge ball players.

November 5, 1904 – The *Globe* reported that the pygmies living in the International Village at the World's Fair saw an airship (balloon) and wanted to buy one. They were convinced it would make them great elephant hunters. They asked one official to negotiate for them and promised they would pay him with the first set of tusks. Doesn't this sound like the beginning of a silly movie? Can you imagine these tiny

people fighting a herd of gigantic elephants as they fly overhead and hang under a hot air balloon? Would they use spears? How would they get down to the

Airship at the 1904 Fair

elephants after they killed them? I think this needs to become a funny movie.

November 6, 1904 – Immigration officials were looking into rumors that the Chinese who were "on exhibit" at the World's Fair were gathering weapons. It was reported that there had already been several escape attempts and that they might refuse to go home. Life was pretty bad in China back then. I'll bet that, when they saw how well people in America lived, they really were tempted to try and stay here. That part is still true over a hundred years later.

November 19, 1904 – A fire destroyed the Missouri Pavilion at the World's Fair two weeks before it was to close. Most of the treasures inside were saved. The U.S. Marines rushed in to save the bell that Missourians had bought with their donations for the USS Missouri. Many of you have seen that bell on display in the museum on the lower level of the State Capitol Building.

November 26, 1904 – President Teddy Roosevelt was back in St. Louis and visiting the World's Fair on this day. He met with Geronimo and was entertained by the famous cowboy comedian, Will Rogers.

December 1, 1904 – David Francis said, "Farewell to all thy splendor." and threw a switch closing the World's Fair. It was a splendid thing for sure but all good things must come to an end. However, this fair is still giving people all sorts of things to think about and still gives us some very good mysteries waiting to be solved.

May 11, 1906 – A huge crowd was on hand to see the World's Fair Ferris Wheel blown up. To this day no one knows what happened to it. Some of it's steel parts were taken away on railroad flatcars and melted down for recycling. Surprisingly, it's the very biggest parts that can't be found.

For instance the huge hub of the wheel is the largest piece of iron ever cast in one piece. It wouldn't fit on any railway car. So what did they do with it? No one knows! Some say it is buried there in Forest Park. If you would use a metal detector and find that thing under the ground, you would be famous. It is such an important item that it would be worth a lot of money.

Good Old Pollution

Today our politicians tell us that high gasoline prices are good for us. They will force us to use more trains, subways, and busses. They don't want to think about those of us who don't have trains, subways, and busses coming to our houses. They have always done stuff like that. If they don't know how to fix a problem they will tell us that it's really a good thing or it's good for us.

For many years St. Louis was a city with many factories and many homes all heated with coal and coal also powered the factories and trains all through the city. Black coal smoke was everywhere. People had trouble breathing. Laundry hung out to dry soon turned gray and everything was a sad and depressing dark dingy disgusting mess.

In 1870, Mayor Nathan Cole said, "The smoke will roll heavenward from her (the city's) furnaces, mill, machine shops, and factories. – and shall cover like a silver sheen her hills and valleys far and near." How's that for a pretty promise? The air full of smoke and everything far and near covered with dust and soot. Thanks, Mr. Mayor.

The streets were a problem also. They were always muddy and of course before cars the streets were filled with horses and mules. So the mud wasn't just plain old mud. It was mud you didn't want to step in. In 1873 the store owners and merchants in St. Louis organized a ferry service just to take people across the street. That's right – it wasn't a ferry to take people across the river but just across the street! At Third and Washington Streets where the so-called mud flowed "deepest and most rapid." Shoppers and merchants would step aboard the ferry boat and be pulled across the street by ropes.

In 1875 they actually tried to solve the problem of the muddy streets. One plan was to hang water pipes twenty feet above the streets and sprinkle the streets when they got too filthy. Think about this. How ugly would those pipes be? What about the people below the pipes when they were turned on? And one more thing – Wait until you read the next story about what was in that water!

A St. Louis newspaper was happy to report in 1902 that a new invention called the automobile was going to result in "a more perfect state of public health." Well, I suppose the automobiles didn't drop piles of stuff in the streets but it's funny to think that now everyone tells us the internal combustion engine and fossil fuels are terrible. Back then they hoped the cars would make the city cleaner.

But four years later things weren't getting any better. In November of 1906 people were heating up their homes and the air was getting thick. Schools had to be closed because of air pollution. Most places didn't have electricity yet so schools had to depend on sunlight coming in the windows for the kids to read and do their work. The smoke over the city was so bad that the sunlight was blocked out!

In 1923 the air pollution was so bad in St. Louis that the Missouri Botanical Garden made plans to move out of town. They bought a large tract of land in Gray Summit, Missouri for that purpose. Today that's a popular place first known as the Shaw Arboretum and now, as the Shaw Nature Reserve.

A Chamber of Commerce official in St. Louis was trying to tell people that air pollution was a good thing in 1923. He said, "We can only hope that visitors will regard each piece of soot as evidence of our industry."

The next year the smoke and smog were so bad in St. Louis that cars were crashing and thieves were committing hold-ups while "broad daylight" was actually darkness. Folks on the sidewalks of St. Louis carried umbrellas because the air pollution was so bad. The soot would attract water droplets in the air and fall as large and small globs of black goo on everyone below.

In 1932 the Great Depression was going on and people were forced to burn cheap coal in their homes and businesses. This cheap coal had more sulfur and other bad stuff in it and it made the air pollution much worse. Other people burned wood which didn't make such bad smoke but it make more of it. It made the sky so dark that the street lights had to be on all day long.

Some Depression-poor people had moved into Forest Park and were digging a very low-grade coal from the ground.

They would stay on and live in the holes. Selling the coal for pennies and living in the holes – for them life was truly the pits.

November 28, 1939 came to be known as "Black Tuesday" in St. Louis. A cloud of thick smoke covered the downtown area. The street lights had to be turned on but traffic was still snarled and there were lots of car wrecks because, even with the street lights and headlights, drivers still couldn't see where they were going.

Do remember when I said that politicians would rather tell us that bad things are good than to do something to actually solve the problems? They think solving problems might inconvenience the voters and they (the politicians) will lose some votes. That's why this air pollution thing went on for so many years. But finally, on February 24, 1940, a man stepped forward with a plan. Mayor Raymond Tucker presented his plan to end the air pollution problems. Many others objected but he was able to start his plan and he was extremely successful. Today one of the biggest streets in St. Louis is named for this brave problem solver.

Don't Drink the Water!

Today St. Louis and its metropolitan area have some of the best drinking water in the world. The people who make soda, beer, and all sorts of food here get awards all the time and one reason is the good water in the city. But it wasn't always that way.

Back in 1888 everyone was complaining about finding eels in their sinks. Imagine turning on your water faucet and the water coming out has eels in it! The Water Commissioner said that eels and minnows could easily pass through the filters when they were young and then they would grow while they lived in the settling basins. But he said not to worry about it. He claimed that they don't harm the water – they actually make it better!

In 1895 they had another problem. There was a different kind of critter appearing in the drinking water. They were little crabs! The Health commissioner told people that this was really a good thing. He reminded them that the drinking water used to be so muddy than no one could see the creatures but now the water is clearer than it used to be. Weren't the people lucky?

In 1900 things were getting serious. Millions of visitors were expected to come to St. Louis for the World's Fair and there wasn't even good drinking water for them. It was so embarrassing! An important group of people went out to St. James, Missouri and tasted the nice clean water in the Upper Meramec River. They said it tasted like nectar but couldn't think of any way to get enough of it to St. Louis.

In 1902 people were still worried but couldn't seem to find a solution to the need for clean water. That spring one leader said, "We have reached the time of year when our water turns from the milky gray of winter to a warm chocolate color."

In 1903 there was more bad news. A trace element showed up in St. Louis drinking water. It was part of a secret test. The trace element had been put into a sewage canal in Chicago and here it was in St. Louis.

You see, for years Chicago had been dumping sewage and poisons into the Illinois River and sending the stuff downstream. People in places like Peoria and St. Louis complained but the folks in Chicago said there was no way that Chicago pollution could affect anything as far away as St. Louis. This test proved that Chicago sewage was in the St. Louis water.

Of course there is a happy ending to the story. On March 21, 1904, just a few days before the opening of the World's Fair, St. Louis got a new water purification system. Now St. Louis water no longer had "body" or eels or crabs or that nice chocolate color.

The True Story of the Creeping Boulder Boogers!

You've probably never heard of it because it was never in North America before. But now, it has come to Missouri and a few other states and it's spreading rapidly. Here are some things you should know about rock snot:

- It is disgusting!
- It grows at a furious rate.
- It kills fish and other water creatures.
- It threatens rivers and streams everywhere.
- It sprouts tendrils and reaches out for new places to grow.

Most people call this gross and disgusting slime, rock snot but its scientific name is Didymosphenia geminate. Scientists and naturalists usually shorten that big name to "Didymo." It's a type of algae that used to exist only in Africa

129

and Asia. It seems to be spreading on the shoes, boots, and waders of fishermen and other people who go from one stream to another.

Didymo Rock Snot is the disgusting slime that's Invading our Missouri streams and rivers.

You've seen the green pond scum that floats on top of our ponds and lakes. Rock snot is sort of like that but it lives on the rocks and mud at the bottom of the water. Like the pond scum, this is a type of algae but this kind eventually covers the entire bottom of the body of water and keep the fish and other creatures for their food supply.

As bad as it seems for our fishing streams, it could be even worse. If or when this stuff gets into big rivers like the Missouri or the Mississippi, it can clog the rivers and mess up barge traffic. It could even reach the big cities and clog their water intakes which would shut off the drinking water supply for places like St. Louis and Kansas City! It could also grow up through the sewer pipes and make its way toward our rain gutters or even our toilets. Imagine what a city would be like if tens of thousands of toilets were clogged with this slime and couldn't flush.

Here's an idea. So far no one has been able to figure out a way to stop this stuff. You could become rich and famous if you could find a way to control it. Algae is just a simple little plant so there should be some way to outsmart it. You could go down in history as the person who saved the world from the snot-a-thon!

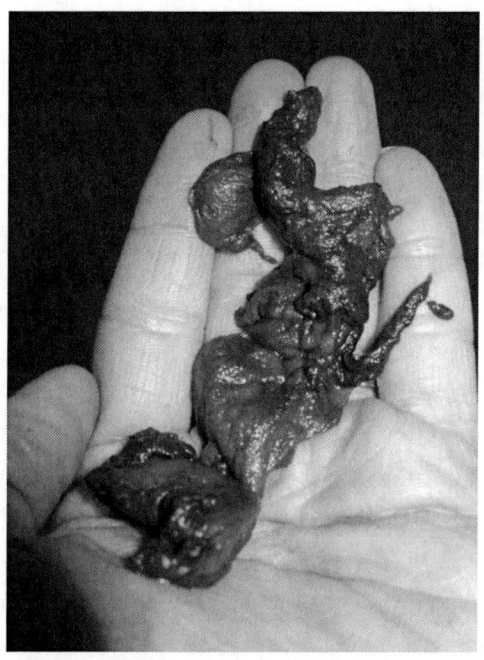

The new (small) chunks of rock snot are commonly called "boulder boogers."

What starts as an invisible micro-organism stuck to someone's shoe soon turns into a boulder booger. But this is actually a new colony just getting started. Soon the boulder booger is a disgusting mass of slime and ooze that's trying to choke an entire river or stream.

For right now, what can we do to stop this stuff? Well, that's it – just stop it. Try to keep it from spreading because no one knows how to get rid of it. We need to keep it from spreading into new territories until someone can find a way to kill it. Rock snot sounds awful but the truth is that it's actually much worse than it sounds.

Strange Sports Events

High School Football Hauntings

There must be a couple of dozen high schools in Missouri which are reported to be haunted. Just about all of them seem to have a football player who died in a game or at practice then he won't go away. He just wanders around playing pranks or showing up and then disappearing. Several of them supposedly had their football fields built on top of an Indian graveyard. I'm not really convinced about any of these stories. Sometimes stories are just fun to tell and I think some high school kids made up some good ones and the modern high school kids enjoy passing the stories along.

There is one High School haunting that makes a better story than most of them. Up in the St. Joseph area is a great old school called Benton High School. Guess what? – It was said to be built on an old Indian burial spot. During the evening hours, people who find themselves on the third floor have complained about "something" up there throwing books and someone screams and yells but no one is there. They also say that a strange voice comes on the intercom but no one is in the office to talk in the intercom.

Here's a part you'll like. The school secretary from long ago is said to be still on the job. She has been seen walking into the main office and people say they have recognized the aroma of her distinctive perfume. She doesn't do anything bad – she's just there. That's enough. I don't remember any school secretaries who might have been dead but I do remember a school nurse who was old enough that we might have been suspicious.

In a newer part of the building there has been reported a red light that floats up and down the long hallways. Once an "apparition" was said to enter a classroom, turn on a television set and sit down to watch a show. I'll bet it watched the Adams Family.

Benton High School

Something to think about: My old high school had a strange thing happen year after year after year. No matter how many points the baseball, or basketball, or football team would score, the team from the other town would always score several more.

Do you think we might have been playing on an old Indian burial site? That's my story and I'm sticking with it!

Kansas City's Kemper Arena

Kemper Arena has been the scene of many kinds of events. One popular attraction was always wrestling. As you may know, the wrestlers do all sorts of stunts to create interest and draw in their fans. Well, on May 23, 1999, a popular wrestler named Owen Hart planned to make an entrance into the wrestling ring by being lowered from the steel rafters on a cable. This was kind of amazing because Owen was afraid of heights.

Then, you guessed it – something broke and Owen Hart fell to his death right there in front of everyone! Now some folks claim that his ghost haunts the Arena. Workers there say that they see him, still dressed in the blue jacket he wore that night, walking around in the rafters. Some say that for a moment his cable appears. Whenever these things happen, the lights are said to flicker off and on.

If you're ever lucky enough to go to an event at the Kemper Arena and the lights start to blink, quick – look up into the rafters!

The Late Owen Hart

Hunting and Fishing in Zombie Country

In October, 2012 the Missouri Department of Conservation posted an important warning on their website. It warned of a new invasive species of animals in Missouri – ZOMBIES! The following information was taken from their official webpage so read it carefully and be careful out there!

They advise us that hunters and campers in the outdoors should realize that there is always a chance that they might encounter a zombie while out in the field. A wise person will be prepared and know what to do if you run into the walking dead.

They say that organized zombie hunts are not a good idea because it might interfere with the other hunters in the woods. Also, large groups of zombie hunters could stir up zombie swarms and make the situation even worse than it already is. We should just let the sleeping dead lie.

Being able to identify the zombies when we see them is important. After all, we wouldn't want to battle innocent people who were nothing more than just creepy and ugly. Here are some good ways to recognize the undead.

- They usually have grayish-green dull skin.
- They often wear inappropriate clothing for the season or terrain (no coat or shoes, for instance or maybe a ragged business suit in the forest).
- They almost always have open wounds, other injuries like missing or damaged limbs but they're not bleeding.

- Zombies do not respond to verbal stimulus or exhibit any interest in their immediate surroundings.
- **The biggest clue is this: The thing is trying to eat you.**

If you know what zombies eat, you can learn to avoid them. If they don't see you, they won't bother you. You must understand the zombies love meat and brains. They especially love those of humans but fish and wildlife are also good sources of nourishment for them.

We tend to think of zombies stalking populated areas but there are also plenty of them in the rural areas as well. Scientific observations tend to indicate that it's food that makes them move from one place to another and also that they don't like being alone. They prefer to travel in packs or swarms when they are on the move.

It also seems clear that zombies don't like cold weather. After the first hard frost, rural zombies may "hibernate" under leaf litter or even under water until the spring thaw.

Whether you are hunting, hiking, fishing, mountain biking, or any other outdoor activity, here are some things that the Department of Conservation Web Page suggests to help you make it back alive:

- Always let someone know where you are going before you leave home. Also tell them when you expect to return. It's a good idea to leave a map or GPS coordinates with your family.
- Avoid cauliflower fields or gardens with cauliflowers. Since cauliflowers look like brains, they often lure

zombies. (You may want to remind the ladies in your school's lunch rooms about this fact.)

- Meat processing plants, butcher shops, and other areas of concentrated meat and brains can attract zombies.

- If you encounter a large pack of zombies, try to escape rather than fighting them alone. While you may be able to run faster, remember that zombies are relentless at pursuit. Run, hide, and call 9-1-1.

- If in the suburban outdoors, remember that shopping malls and big-box stores may serve as fortresses against the walking dead, but they can also attract zombies in large numbers.

Remember, cauliflowers look like brains and
they may attract swarms of zombies!

Hunters have found that, in the woods, tree stands are good positions for escaping roaming zombies, but remember that free-standing tree stands can be knocked down by a small pack of zombies. Follow manufacturers' instructions when setting up your stand. And it may be possible that some especially nimble zombies may be able to climb tree stands.

Remember to always wear a safety harness in your tree stand. The Department of Conservation warns: "Falling from a tree stand can injure you or make you dead. **Falling from a tree stand into the gaping maw of a zombie can make you undead.**"

You can stay cool when you are safely
harnessed in your tree stand.

Duck and goose hunters beware. Zombies do not need air. They can stay submerged underwater for long periods of time. The M.D.C. tries to keep all waterfowl areas zombie-free but we should still use caution. They suggest that people wading in murky waters should wear a shark suit over their hunting clothes. They seem to think that, like sharks, zombies cannot bite through the steel mesh shark suit.

Dogs are good hunting partners and are usually "very sensitive to zombies." They will usually bark and growl when a zombie is near. However, dogs cannot sense zombies which are submerged under the water. Be careful and don't let your dog come into direct contact with a zombie. The M.D.C. says, **"Don't let man's best friend turn into man's worst friend."**

Lumberjacks, hunters, and others in the woods need to know the following things if they ever should encounter a swarm or even a single zombie:

- Chainsaws axes and machetes are excellent weapons against zombies. **Remember that a severed zombie head can still bite**.
- Controlled fire can be a slow weapon but still a good one for stopping zombies. However to completely do away with a zombie, you must completely burn him leaving no trace or use explosives to blow him to smithereens.
- When you are fighting against zombies, you should be sure to wear the proper clothing. The best anti-zombie gear will keep you from getting splashed with blood or brains. After all, that is how people often get the zombie virus.

Finally, here is a good simple warning note to fishermen. If you should get a zombie on your hook, CUT THE LINE!

****

This article was inspired by the good-natured Halloween spoof from the Missouri Department of Conservation. Now we know – they not only do a good job with our natural resources, but they also have a great sense of humor.

Strange News

Strange Gleanings

Some things aren't big stories but they are pretty strange little things that really happened. This section is made of things gleaned from newspapers, magazines, television news, and books. These are all taken from my book, <u>This Day in Missouri History</u>.

- **December 14, 1763** – This is the birthday of Joseph Conway for whom Conway Road in St. Louis County is named. This Indian fighter was said by Ripley's to have been tomahawked three times, shot three times, and left for dead three times. He was one tough dude!

- **October 10, 1764** – The sad remains of the Missouri Tribe appeared at St. Louis on this day. The 400 Indians for whom our state was named demanded that they be allowed to live in the town. They demanded provisions and then stole them. Most of the colonists fled across the Mississippi until Pierre Laclede talked the Indians into leaving.

- **January 3, 1787** – Birthday of mountain man, William S. "Old Bill" Williams. A fur trapper, guide, and Protestant preacher, he lived with the Osage and Ute Indians but came back to Kansas City where he spent his final years and was buried. Old Bill was so tough that Kit Carson is said to have warned people not to step in front of him when he was hungry. John C. Fremont went so far as to accuse him of being a cannibal. He was so wild looking that his own granddaughter would hide from him.

- **June 3, 1812** – Imagine the scene: A terrible storm followed by a dense fog and a downtown St. Louis church bell began ringing with no one touching the rope. Residents fell to their knees and prayed. What could it mean? First the storm and then no one could see anything in the terrible dense fog. And then the bell was ringing but no one was in the church or pulling on the bell's rope. What was making the bell ring – and why? When the fog lifted they saw a rope running from the bell to another church belfry across the street. Now that was a good trick!

- **January 15, 1814** – The Missouri Gazette carried an advertisement for what seems to be the first live entertainment in the state's history. A magician claimed to present a "Spectacle of recreative sports, of Mathematicks, and Phisicks." Among other things, he promised to cut the head off a chicken then fix it back like new.

- **June 9, 1819** – The *Western Engineer* arrived in St. Louis. A most unusual boat! Called "Long's Dragon," it was built to travel up the Missouri and it was shaped and painted to resemble a huge serpent. Smoke and steam came from its mouth and nostrils. Intended to intimidate the Indians, it did that very well.

- **June 21, 1819** – The Steamboat, *Western Engineer*, (that most folks called "Long's Dragon") left St. Louis on this date headed upstream to Franklin and beyond. Read more about this in Tales From Missouri and the Heartland.

- **October 2, 1820** – In the "State Capital Building" which was the Missouri Hotel in St. Louis, Missouri's first two US Senators were selected on this day. (David Barton and Thomas Hart Benton) The deciding vote was cast by Daniel Ralls from Pike County and for whom Ralls County is named. He was so ill on October 2nd that he had to be carried, still in his bed, to the meeting of the Legislature. He died four days later. Hearing of his father's death, a son came to St. Louis to claim the body but no body or burial place could be found.

- **November 18, 1824** – This is the birthday of the "retreating general." Franz Sigel, a leader of the German community in St. Louis he organized a regiment of Union soldiers. He retreated at Carthage, Wilson's Creek, and again at Pea Ridge. Each time he retreated from a battle, he was promoted.

- **December 28, 1831** – Rev. Isaac McCoy, a Baptist missionary to the Indians, brought his family to western Missouri on this date. His son, John C. McCoy, would first establish Westport, MO and then Kansas City. You will read more about John C. in a few seconds.

- **September 22, 1842** – James Shields and Abraham Lincoln came to Missouri to fight a duel. Shields, an Illinois attorney and State Auditor accused Lincoln of writing a newspaper article critical of him. For weapons they chose cavalry sabers but Lincoln convinced Shields that he did not write the article so the duel was called off. Shields probably also noticed that Lincoln's long arms gave him a much longer reach.

- **October 24, 1844** – A tornado struck the cabin of Kansas City pioneer, John Calvin McCoy. It picked up his three-month-old son, bed and all, and carried him out of his house. He was later found, still in his bed, and safe.

- **November 26, 1848** – The Great Pathfinder, John C. Fremont, "Old Bill" Williams and other Missourians chose the wrong pass and became stranded in a severe Rocky Mountain winter. At one point the men thought they saw green grass in the snow. It turned out to be the <u>tops</u> of evergreen trees! Eleven men died on that trip and Old Bill was accused of cannibalism.

- **October 19, 1865** – The Missouri Democrat newspaper was reporting that a trapper, James Lumley, had seen a "bright luminous body" in the skies moving toward the east. Then there was a loud explosion and the smell of sulfur in the air. He found the large object which was divided into compartments and had something like hieroglyphs on its surface. He also discovered glass & "strange stains."

- **July 15, 1869** – The *Missouri Weekly Patriot* in Springfield reported that Mat Harbert of Cassville sent his wife and children to the loft because a grizzly bear was in the wheat field. Once his family was safe, the brave Mr. Harbert shot the monster and then moved in for a closer look. The grizzly bear turned out to have been his mule.

- **November 11, 1870** – A railroad bridge being built across the Missouri at St. Charles collapsed killing nineteen and injuring many more. This was the first of many disasters involving that bridge.

- **March 27, 1871** – St. Louis was reporting about 4000 infant deaths each year and local physicians on this day blamed contaminated milk from local dairies.

- **August 11, 1872** – An astronomer predicted that a comet was coming and would hit St. Louis. Many people panicked and many left town. Can you imagine how frightened everyone was? Then, just to make things even worse some young boys stood on street corners, and every so often pointed to the sky and yelled, "Here she comes!"

- **July 2, 1875** – A weather service log book reported "a small shower of bullfrogs" in St. Louis. This was the actual weather report but the report didn't say what caused the frog shower. Do you think maybe a tornado passed through a pond or marsh picking up the critters?

- **March 8, 1877** – The *Neosho Times* reported that in Washburn a show was in progress in which one performer asked people to shoot at him with a rifle. He would then catch the bullet with a stick. Instead, he caught it with the side of his head. Oops!

- **April 11, 1877** – On this night, fireman Phelim O'Toole became a legend. The Southern Hotel was on fire and about a dozen people were trapped on upper floors, so high that the ladders couldn't reach them. O'Toole swung on a rope to reach tied-together bed sheets then climbed up the sheets and brought all the people to safety. Thankful St. Louis citizens awarded O'Toole a check for $500.00. He was such a great guy that he didn't even keep the reward but immediately donated all the money to an orphan's fund.

- **July 6, 1880** – Fireman, Phelim O'Toole was putting out a routine small fire when the extinguisher in his hands blew up and killed him. Over 20,000 people lined the route of his funeral procession. Remember, O'Toole was the St. Louis hero who saved so many people by swinging to and from their hotel windows on bed sheets.

- **December 8, 1881** – A railroad bridge across the Missouri at St. Charles collapsed. This was the third time! Thirty one freight cars plunged into the river. It was also proving to be a hazard for steamboats as several boats had already crashed into the bridge and several more would later.

- **November 20, 1885** – Who's the fairest of them all? At this date in St. Louis the fairest of all was the beautiful socialite, Kate Brewington Bennett. This toast of society was envied for her lily-white complexion. They didn't know that she had been taking small amounts of arsenic to keep herself pale. She didn't know that arsenic was a poison if it accumulated in your system. She is buried in Bellefontaine Cemetery.

- **July 26, 1892** – "Houses Demolished—Railroad Tracks and Trains Swallowed Up—Several Persons Killed and Injured—Miraculous Escapes and Rescues" read the headlines after the Mill Creek Sewer Explosion in St. Louis.

- **May 11, 1894** – The horrific Meeks Family Murder of Linn County. This subject of songs and ballads saw the Meeks family axed to death but one severely-injured seven-year-old survived to identify her attackers. There's much more to this incredible story!

- **April 9, 1899** – Birthday of James McDonnell, founder of McDonnell Aircraft Corp. in St. Louis. James McDonnell's previous job was with Henry Ford where he developed the famous Ford Tri-Motor planes but Ford fired him for wearing knickers at work. In 1939 he opened his own aircraft company at Lambert Field. I think Henry Ford made a big mistake! This reminds us of the time when Walt Disney was fired by the *Kansas City Star* newspaper because Disney had absolutely no creativity at all. A short time later the creative genius, Disney, bought the *Kansas City Star*.

- **April 22, 1900** – There used to be a military museum on South Broadway in St. Louis. But on this day in 1900 a tour guide was showing visitors an artillery shell from the Spanish American war and explaining how powerful it was when he accidentally dropped it and blew up the museum!

- **January 13, 1904** – Nine boys and one man were killed in St. Louis at the Brown Shoe Company. It was quitting time and people were pushing and shoving to get home. They rushed onto an elevator which was actually one floor up above them at the time. The victims fell six stories.

- **April 26, 1907** – Two volunteer firemen were killed and eight injured when a building blew up in Luxemburg (St. Louis County). The fire was set by arsonists and no one realized the building was full of dynamite. That was a really bad surprise!

- **May 11, 1910** – When the steamboat, *City of Saltillo* punctured its hull on a rock near Glen Park, MO, women and children were allowed off the sinking boat first. However, the boat hadn't yet reached the shore and the ladies were crowded off the gangplank into the Mississippi. Five women and a baby died but the gallant men with the good manners were all OK.

- **February 17, 1911** – Public school students in St. Louis were receiving lunch each day for one cent. This penny lunch consisted of a jelly sandwich and a piece of caramel candy. On this date the school board was considering a new five cent lunch "which would be sufficient to divert the small boy's attention from his appetite to his books."

- **July 11, 1911** – Missouri history that was not made: The Cardinals were on their way to Boston and their sleeping cars were toward the front of the train. The engine was so noisy that the team complained and their cars were moved to the rear of the train. That night the train crashed down an embankment and the front cars were all destroyed killing 14. Cardinal players helped to rescue survivors but none of the players were injured.

- **November 10, 1912** – The *Post-Dispatch* reported on something known as the "St. Louis Death Reel." Albert Bond Lambert had a motion picture film of aviation pioneers taken at a flying contest at Kinloch Field earlier in the year. Seven of the people on the film had since died. Another, Teddy Roosevelt, had been recently wounded in an assassination attempt. It definitely seemed like bad luck to be in that movie!

- **August 7, 1915** – Miller Huggins, the Cardinals Manager was coaching third base with runners on when the Brooklyn Trolley Dodgers sent a rookie pitcher to the mound. Huggins told the young pitcher that he wanted to inspect the baseball and the rookie tossed it to him. The Cardinals runner on third then scored. No one had called "time out."

- **April 13, 1934** – Chimps at the St. Louis Zoo were learning a new show and were being taught hand signals and signs for driving small cars. The zoo considered a publicity stunt of having the chimps get actual Missouri drivers licenses.

- **January 25, 1959** – Drunken pigeons? The St. Louis Health and Hospital Director announced a plan to get swarms of pigeons drunk on alcohol-soaked bread crumbs. The drunken birds would then be scooped up and hauled off to the city pound's gas chamber. Bird lovers killed the plan instead of the birds.

- **April 23, 1967** – On this day James Earl Ray hid in a bread bin aboard a bakery truck and escaped from Missouri's State Penitentiary. Less than a year later he killed Dr. Martin Luther King

- **August 21, 1967** – Gov. Hearnes had complained about the starlings at the Governor's Mansion. So on this day five men shot and killed 2000 of those pesky birds on and around the Mansion Grounds. It turned out that the birds were not starlings at all but purple martins, a valuable species protected by state and federal law. Oops!

- **July 19, 1972** – MoMo the "Missouri Monster" was born (first sighted) on this day in Louisiana, MO. Having inspired a country song and a ride at Six Flags and who knows what else, some local high school students admitted to wearing a fake fur coat and carrying out the hoax.

- **November 22, 1980 –** Kenneth Swyers of Overland slid down the north leg of the Arch to his death. He had parachuted to the top of the Arch as a publicity stunt. But the wind caught his chute, and he started to fall. He became tangled in his parachute cords and tumbled down the side crashing into the pavement below.

- **May 23, 1997** – The paddlefish became the official aquatic animal of Missouri. The primitive fish thrives in the Mississippi, Missouri, and Osage Rivers and our larger lakes.

- **May 23, 1997** – The channel catfish was chosen as our official fish. Adults can grow very large!

- **November 11, 2011** – On this date, 11-11-11, about 125 UFOs were reported over the Kansas City metropolitan area. These orange globes would appear, divide, and fly through the sky over K.C., Independence, Raytown, and Lee's Summit.

- **May 25, 2012** – Residents of Blue Springs, Missouri had been reporting unidentified lights in the sky for two weeks and now a television news crew saw and recorded the objects. Blue Springs is near Belton and the areas mentioned just above.

What do you think?

In this book we have seen many examples of strange and sometimes mysterious happenings around our state. What do you think some explanations might be?

Of course some of these things were just practical jokes and pranks. I love a good hoax if it doesn't hurt anyone. And some of these things were great! Sometimes a prank can backfire on you such as the dark night when a boy I know was trying to scare his sisters. He made things so scary that he scared himself. In fact he was so frightened that he wet his pants!

But some pranks are good clean fun. No one gets hurt but everyone gets to look back on the situation and have a good laugh. MoMo the monster was a great example of that. People in more than twenty counties let their imaginations get carried away and it was just some boys a hundred miles away in a fake fur coat. Other people like the local store owners, the radio host who wrote a song, and many other people across the state enjoyed thinking about the creature. We do love a mystery don't we?

In the Ozarks some old timers will tell you that, "Some people would climb a tree to tell a lie when truth would do on the ground." They're just pointing out to us that some people love to tell lies. They really enjoy fooling us and will go out of their way to do so. So, many of the spooky things around us might very well be those practical jokes and stories that people tell us just to get us all worked up.

People who are more serious about all of this might tell us that there is another dimension parallel to ours and spirits can cross back and forth when they want to or need to. That would explain how the mother in one story came back from the dead to help her sick children. It might also explain how and why some of the houses we mentioned have such strange things happening in them.

Is there a parallel dimension or a parallel universe? If someone tells you that they know for sure, then they are not telling you the truth. It might be more accurate if they tell you that they <u>think</u> there is a parallel dimension or they <u>hope</u> there is a parallel dimension. It's really fun to think about though – isn't it? If it were true then we might someday learn to cross it ourselves. Then we could go over and meet our ancestors. Maybe we could meet people from the Bible or from our history books.

Since we live in three dimensions (length, width, and depth) people say that the fourth dimension is time. If that is true and we learn to cross over, we could go and visit people and places in the past or we could look ahead into the future. You might want to see who you are going to marry. You might want to see what mistakes you will make and avoid making those. It's fun to think about!

If you like the thought of time travel and bending the fourth dimension so you can quickly travel through space, you really should read <u>A Wrinkle in Time</u> by Madeleine L'Engle. It is one of the best stories you will ever read.

Here's one more thought for you. We are constantly learning that the human brain is a wonderful thing and our minds are far more powerful than anyone had ever realized. What if we were able to harness our minds to do things for us like we see in the movies?

What if a few people have already figured out how to do some things that we can't do? Could they be doing mental tricks to frighten us or to make us wonder what just happened? If you could do tricks with your mind, wouldn't you have some fun with it and trick a few people?

I hope that we never figure out what makes all these strange, mysterious, and silly things happen. I hope we never stop giving funny names to animals. I hope that we all can keep a love for mysteries and for scary things. I hope that dark nights will always make us want to tell ghost stories and cause us to get those goose bumps. I hope when you hear a good story, you will write it down and save it. I hope you have a friend or two who like to share these stories with you. I hope you continue to love a good mystery.

Here are some other Missouri books that you are bound to like

To order any Heritage Books: See the following page or you can visit www.Missouri—Books.com.

Send the books marked below:

Name

_____

Address

_____

City,   State,   Zip

_____

School Edition
Tales From Missouri and the Heartland, number of paperbacks _____

School Edition
Tales From Missouri and the Heartland, number of hard covers _____

Eight Tough Kids (available in hard cover books only) _____

This Day in Missouri History, number of paperbacks _____

This Day in Missouri History, number of hard covers _____

Total number of paperback books _____ X $14.95 = $_____

Total number of hard cover books _____ X $19.95 = $_____

Total number of books _____ X $3.00 Shipping & Handling = $_____

Total enclosed $_____

Thank you! Please make your check payable to Tales from Missouri and send the order to:

Tales From Missouri
1487 Clearview Road
Union, MO 63084-3032